※ Christmas 2008 ※

Dear Ken,

There are a lot of old favorites in here, including Annie's favorite salad! I think you'd find some great crowd-pleasers — apple fritters ... which we should try on a snowy day.

Much love to a budding chef—

Mom

WHAT'S COOKING
CONNECTICUT
SHORELINE?

comfort foods

*A Diverse Collection of Recipes
from Connecticut Shoreline Residents,
Specialty Markets and Inns.*

Diane Gardner
Kim Castaldo
Photographs by Kelley McMahon
Design by Tammy Vaz

Copyright 2007
Diane Gardner
Kim Castaldo
www.whatscookingmadison.com

Photographs by
Kelley McMahon
copyright 2007

Design by
Tammy Vaz

Published by
Jostens, Commercial Publications

ISBN: 978-0-9773675-1-1

Welcome

Two years after embarking on our first adventure together as friends and business partners, we bring to you a new collection of comfort food recipes that have been generously shared by residents, inns and specialty markets from Greenwich to Stonington.

As with our first book, "What's Cooking Madison?" this book is filled with simple recipes that are easy to prepare and delicious. Once again, our book would not have been possible without the outpouring of residents who graciously shared family secrets, traditions and favorites so willingly with us. It is the contributions from the residents and the generosity of the many cheese shops, fish markets, specialty markets and inns that make our book unique and a treasured collection for years to come.

In writing this book, we have found many recipes that we have brought into our homes, and they have become some of our favorites.

As you explore the pages of this book, we hope that you will gain as much pleasure from reading it, as we had in creating it.

Happy Cooking, Diane and Kim

DIANE GARDNER

Diane (Perry) Gardner, formerly of Lake City, South Carolina is married to Bill Gardner and has three children Jesse (15), Ty (14) and Halle (11).

Prior to becoming a full time Mom and Homemaker, Diane enjoyed a successful business career as an Account Executive for Cable Adnet selling advertising on CNN and ESPN in Charlotte, North Carolina. Diane consistently earned the President's award for the highest sales producers in North Carolina. Diane has excelled at everything she sets out to do in her life.

Diane is very active in the Madison community. She has been serving on the board of the Friends of Madison Youth (FOMY) for the past six years and has been serving as co-president of FOMY for the last two years. Diane, along with a dear friend, created and started Hammonassett Moonlight Run, a 5K family run. This is the largest fundraiser for FOMY, a safehaven for teenagers along the shoreline.

"Diane developed a passion for cooking from her grandmother at a very young age, and has shared it with not only our entire family, but everyone she comes in contact with. I love to watch her teach and transfer that passion for cooking to our kids," says her husband, Bill.

Diane has a tremendous skill for entertaining and the ability to make preparing multiple dishes seem effortless. She loves to share that passion and skill with anyone who possesses that same love for cooking and doesn't mind wearing an apron.

Diane is the co-author of "What's Cooking Madison?"

KIM CASTALDO

Kim (Carroll) Castaldo, formerly of Woodbridge, CT is a 1985 graduate of Villanova University. She continues to represent the University today as a member of the school's recruiting network.

Prior to marrying Mark Castaldo, Kim worked for MCI TeleCommunications as a Major Account Representative where she earned several awards as the number one sales person in New England. This made her an honored member of the MCI "President's Inner Circle".

In the early years of her marriage, after leaving MCI, Kim founded Carroll & Company, a sports marketing agency, which produced notable participatory events including; "City Hoops", "Tour de Shore", "Spiketour" and the Hartford edition of the national basketball program "Hoop it Up". She also co-created "Byline '89", a national high school journalism competition sponsored by Pilot Pen and represented the Walter Camp Football Foundation for its 100th anniversary celebration which included the creation of a commemorative book and poster.

Co-author of "What's Cooking Madison?", Kim loves to cook and entertain but is happiest when spending time with her husband and their 4 children; Carolyn, Julianne, Johnny and Connor.

TABLE OF CONTENTS

awesome appetizers

A TRADITIONAL HOLIDAY CHEESE PLATTER

CLAMS CASINO

BRIE PIZZA WITH APPLE-ONION TOPPING

PEPPERONI ROSSI

THE PANTRY'S CARAMELIZED ONION DIP

SALSA BAKED GOAT CHEESE

CHEESY CRISPS

ROASTED EGGPLANT SPREAD WITH CILANTRO AND GARLIC

GINGER DUMPLINGS

CRABMEAT PARTY DIP

MUSSELS IN WHITE WINE

GOAT CHEESE ENDIVE BITES

SPRING ROLLS

GUACAMOLE

TRIOPITA–GREEK CHEESE TURNOVERS

MEL'S RUEBEN DIP

GOUGERES PARSILLACS–CHEESE PUFFS

PORTABELLO MUSHROOMS w/SPINACH, WALNUTS & CHEESE

CHEESE WAFERS–SOUTH CAROLINA STYLE

CAVIAR PIE "DIANE"

CRANBERRY SALSA CRACKERS

OVEN BARBECUED CHICKEN BITES

NANA'S SEAFOOD SALAD

A Traditional
Holiday Cheese Platter

Shared by Fromage Fine Foods & Coffees, Old Saybrook

Suggestions for an easy holiday platter include a variety of cheeses that begin with a mild, soft creamy cheese and extend to a sharp semi-soft to a blue cheese, to an aged Italian-French washed rind type.

Include various accompaniments such as salami, prosciutto, olives and fruit spreads. Also fruit, such as grapes, fresh or dried figs, pears, kiwi and apples.

Add a choice of breads, like mild classic baguettes, crusty whole wheat styles, fruit and nut varieties and focaccia.

Remember to pair aged sheep (brebis) or goat's cheese (chevre) from Spain or Italy with Quince of Italian Mostrda (balsamic fruit chutney) to achieve the perfect cheese accompaniment according to your taste.

Expert Cheese mongers at your favorite local cheese shop are able to assist your selections and satisfy your appetite!

COLE
BARBERA
& sheep. Aged
y red barbera
a sweet finish.

KASSERI
Semi-soft sheep's milk from
Greece. Pleasant, unassertive
sharpness.

RED DRAGON
British pub-style
with mustar...

MUSHROOM
From German...
rich, mushroo...
Double-cr...

...AHAN
...-washed
...urns family
and sticky.

RONCAL
Spanish sheep's milk. Firm
texture. Sharp and olivey.

...TE BASQUE
...s milk cheese from
...yrénées. Nutty and
...ty. Excellent w/fruit.

QUEBEC
CHEDDAR
Aged for 6 years.

LA YERBERA
Aged Spanish goat's milk.
Lively taste. Rind treated
...to olive oil...

FRENCH MUENSTER
Flavorful cow's milk from
France. ...aroma.

CATO CORNER'S
"DRUNK MONK"
Their HOOLIGAN washed with
Merrymonk style — Adds
a delightful sharpness.

CRANBERRY STILTON
ENGLISH WHITE STILTON
RICHLY FRUITED WITH
FRESH SWEET-TART
CRANBERRIES.

SERRA DA ESTRELLA
Raw sheep's milk from
Portugal. Semi-soft. Sharp
and flavorful

FORTIES BLUE

Clams Casino

Shared by Don & Sue Knight, Stamford

3	ounces little neck clams	1	handful parsley, chopped
$^1/_2$	pound bacon		pepper, freshly ground
$^1/_2$	cup olive oil	1	loaf crusty Italian bread
$^1/_2$	head garlic, chopped		

Instructions:

Rinse and clean clams. Open clams with a clam knife and keep all the clam on one half of the shell. Discard the other half. Be sure to open the clams over a baking sheet to catch any escaping clam liquid. Reserve clam liquid. Arrange clams on baking sheet and refrigerate.

Cut bacon in small pieces making about 3 dozen pieces. Cook bacon until soft in a pan. Sauté garlic in olive oil until pieces start to turn an almond color. Remove from heat and pour in a bowl and add chopped parsley. Top each clam with a spoonful of olive oil mixture. Then sprinkle each clam with freshly ground pepper. Add a piece or two of bacon to each clam. Place tray in a preheated oven at 400 degrees and cook until the clams are bubbling and the bacon is crisp. If needed, turn the broiler on for the last couple of minutes to really crisp top of clam.

Serve clams family style from the tray with lots of warm, crusty bread for mopping up!

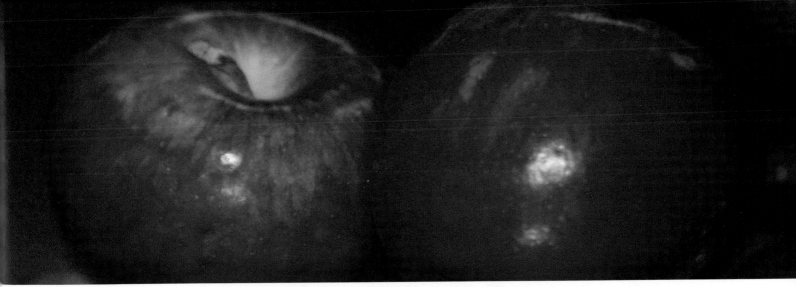

Brie Pizza with Apple-Onion Topping

Shared by Elizabeth Taran, Clinton

2	large onions, sliced thin	1	cup walnuts, toasted
1	tablespoon olive oil	$^1/_2$	teaspoon cinnamon
2	firm apples, peeled and sliced thin	$^1/_4$	teaspoon ground pepper
1	teaspoon sugar	1	14- inch pre-baked pizza shell
2	tablespoons balsamic vinegar	1	8-ounces Brie, cold
$^1/_2$	cup water	$^1/_2$	teaspoon fresh rosemary, chopped

Instructions:

In a large fry pan, sauté onions in olive oil over medium heat, stirring occasionally. Add apples, sugar and vinegar and sauté until soft stirring occasionally and adding water as needed to mixture so it doesn't dry out. You may substitute champagne instead of water. Cook until light brown, about 5 minutes. The water will absorb. Add the walnuts, cinnamon and pepper. Let cool.

Spread apple mixture over pizza dough. Place sliced brie over the apple mixture and sprinkle with rosemary. Bake at 450 degrees for 8–10 minutes or until cheese is melted and pie is hot.

Pepperoni Rossi

Shared by Don Knight, Stamford

5	sweet red peppers	1	bunch fresh basil, rolled and sliced in strips
2	large balls fresh mozzarella, sliced in $1/4$" slices	2	cloves garlic, chopped fine
$1/2$	pound imported prosciutto, sliced paper thin, then sliced in strips	$1/2$	cup olive oil
			kosher salt, to taste
			pepper, to taste

Instructions:

Grill or broil whole peppers until charred on all sides. Place in bowl and cover with plastic wrap. When cool, peel off skin and remove the inside of seeds.

Remove tops of peppers and put 1-2 slices of mozzarella and top with prosciutto slices and cover with basil. Drizzle with olive oil and close pepper. Place stuffed peppers in a corning ware dish, drizzle with the rest of the olive oil and season with kosher salt and pepper. Sprinkle remaining basil strips over the top. Bake at 375 degrees until mozzarella is melted.

Don't forget to dip warm, crusty bread into the juices. *It's a real flavor combination!*

The Pantry's Caramelized Onion Dip

Shared by Andy Rolleri, The Pantry, Fairfield

$1^1/_4$ pounds onions, peeled and sliced thin

$1^1/_2$ ounces butter

$^3/_4$ ounce soy bean oil

8 ounce cream cheese, softened at room temperature

$^1/_2$ tablespoon kosher salt

pinch cayenne pepper

$^1/_4$ tablespoon black pepper

$1^1/_4$ cups sour cream

$1^1/_4$ cups mayonnaise

$^1/_4$ bunch chives, chopped

Instructions:

In a large, heavy skillet over medium heat, slowly caramelize onions in butter and oil until nicely browned. Remove to cutting board and chop coarsely. In a mixer, combine cream cheese, salt, pepper and cayenne with a paddle, until creamy and very soft and smooth. Beat in mayonnaise and sour cream until smooth. Stir in chives and cooled chopped onions. Chill and serve.

Salsa Baked Goat Cheese

Shared by Ann Petroccio, Fairfield

$^1/_4$ cup pine nuts, toasted

1 4 ounce log of goat cheese, softened

3 ounces cream cheese, softened

1 cup roasted tomato salsa

1 tablespoon cilantro, chopped (add more if needed)

tortilla chips, pita chips or toasts

Instructions:

Pre-heat oven to 350 degrees and toast nuts. Cool and place in medium size bowl. Add cheeses and mix well. Scoop into oven safe plate and shape in a disk. Spoon salsa around and on top of cheese disk. Bake for 10-15 minutes and sprinkle with cilantro before serving.

Cheesy Crisps

Shared by Phyllis Carroll, Cape Cod

*These are very popular in Colorado where I lived
for 15 years before coming home to New England.*

$1^3/_4$ cups flour

$^1/_2$ cup yellow cornmeal

$^1/_2$ teaspoon baking soda

$^1/_2$ teaspoon sugar

$^1/_2$ teaspoon salt

$^1/_2$ cup butter, cold

8   ounces extra sharp cheddar
cheese, shredded

2   tablespoons white vinegar

$^2/_3$ cup water

black pepper, coarsely ground

Instructions:

In a large bowl, combine flour, cornmeal, baking soda, sugar and salt with a pastry blender. With a fork, cut in butter until mixture resembles coarse crumbs. Stir in cheese, vinegar and water until mixture forms a soft dough.

Divide into 4 equal parts and wrap separately with plastic wrap. Chill for at least one hour. Grease large baking sheet. On a lightly floured surface, roll 1 ball of dough into a circle, about the size of a pie plate. With a pizza cutter, cut into wedges and place on baking sheet. Wedges will be rough around the edges. Firmly press pepper into dough before baking. Bake at 375 degrees until brown and crispy, about 10 minutes. This is great with guacamole.

Roasted Eggplant Spread with Cilantro and Garlic

Shared by Karen Gilhuly, Milford

$^1/_2$ cup olive oil

2 tablespoons garlic, minced

1 teaspoon lemon juice

$^1/_2$ teaspoon cumin

1 tablespoon kosher salt

1 teaspoon pepper, freshly ground

2 medium sized eggplants, seeded, cut into $^3/_4$ inch cubes

4 red peppers, seeded, cut into $^1/_2$ inch cubes

1 large red onion, cut into $^3/_4$ inch cubes

1 large Vidalia onion, cut into $^3/_4$ inch cubes

3 tablespoons cilantro, freshly chopped

salt, to taste

pepper, to taste

3 tablespoons parsley, chopped

Instructions:

In a large bowl, combine olive oil, garlic, lemon juice, cumin, salt and pepper. Add all vegetables and toss to coat. Spray 2 baking sheets with non stick cooking spray and spread vegetables out on sheets. Roast vegetables in a 425 degree oven for 30 minutes or until cooked through. Remove from oven and let cool for at least 30 minutes. Transfer vegetables to a food processor and pulse on and off to form a rough puree. Transfer to a bowl and chill for a few hours or over night. Prior to serving, top with cilantro and salt and pepper as desired. This is wonderful served with Cheesy Crisps on page 14.

Ginger Dumplings

Shared by Merry Esposito, Madison

This recipe comes from a Chinese cooking class that I enjoyed taking. They require some work but are well worth it! Best to make the dipping sauce a day ahead to allow the flavors to blend.

1 pound pork, ground	**Dipping sauce**
2 eggs	$1/2$ cup soy sauce
6 scallions, diced	1 tablespoon rice wine vinegar
4 teaspoons fresh ginger, grated	1 tablespoon rice wine
1 teaspoon salt	1 tablespoon ginger, grated
$1/2$ teaspoon brown sugar	1 clove garlic, minced
$1/2$ teaspoon sesame oil	2 scallions, chopped fine
1 package wonton skins	
4 tablespoons oil	

Instructions:

In a large bowl, mix together the pork, eggs, scallions, ginger, salt, brown sugar and sesame oil. Fill each wonton wrapper with 1 tablespoon of the pork filling. Fold the wrapper in half to make a triangle, if the edges don't stay sealed, dampen your fingertips with water and press edges together. Be sure to keep wonton skins moist with a wet paper towel, while waiting to be filled, they can easily dry out. Working in batches, fry the wontons in oil over medium high heat for one minute per side. When the batch is golden brown, add $1/2$ cup of hot water to the skillet. Cover the skillet with a lid and let the wontons steam for 4 minutes. Serve warm with dipping sauce.

Crabmeat Party Dip

Shared by Josephine Redding, Stamford
This is an all time favorite which appears at our family parties.

6	ounces cream cheese	1	small onion, chopped
2	6$\frac{1}{2}$ ounce cans white crab meat, drained	2	teaspoons lemon juice
1	cup Hellman's mayonnaise	$\frac{1}{2}$	teaspoon Tabasco sauce or hot pepper sauce

Instructions:

Pre-heat oven to 350 degrees. Blend cream cheese until smooth and stir in the remaining ingredients. Spoon mixture into oven proof dish (deep round) and bake for 20 minutes or until the top is golden brown and bubbling.

Serve warm with chips or chopped vegetables.

Mussels in White Wine

Shared by Baurle's Bed and Breakfast, Westbrook
Another favorite of Chef Jay, he often serves this over pasta and turns it into a fantastic dinner!

3	pounds mussels		white wine
$\frac{1}{4}$	cup butter		bouquet garni, your choice of herbs*
1	medium onion, finely chopped		
2-3	cloves garlic, chopped	1	tablespoon flour
$\frac{2}{3}$	cup water	4	tablespoons cream
2	tablespoons lemon juice pinch of finely grated lemon rind	2-3	tablespoons fresh parsley, chopped

Instructions:

Thoroughly wash all mussels and discard any open ones. In large sauce pan, melt $\frac{1}{2}$ of the butter, add onions and garlic, sauté. Add wine, water, lemon juice, rind and bouquet garni. Bring to a boil cover and simmer 5 minutes. Add mussels and simmer 5 more minutes, stirring frequently. Take out bouquet and any unopened mussels. In a small bowl, blend the remaining butter with flour and whisk into broth, simmer 2-3 more minutes or until broth thickens slightly. Add cream and $\frac{1}{2}$ the parsley, stir in gently for 1 minute. Serve with warm, crusty bread for dipping!

* bouquet garni—a bunch of herbs, tied together in a cheesecloth to add flavor to broths, soups or stews.

Goat Cheese Endive Bites

Shared by Adam Calkins, Lyme

8	ounces crème fraiche	3	tablespoons chives, chopped
4	ounces fresh goat cheese	3	radishes, sliced finely
4	ounces aged goat cheese, softened	2	heads Belgian endive, outer leaves discarded

Instructions:

Blend together crème fraiche, both goat cheeses and two tablespoons of the chives until completely smooth. Arrange endive leaves on a platter and using a pastry bag fitted with a fluted tip, fill each endive leave with 1 teaspoon of the cheese filling. Top with a slice of radish and sprinkle with remaining chives. Other garnish options include pearls of fresh unpasteurized salmon or sturgeon caviar.

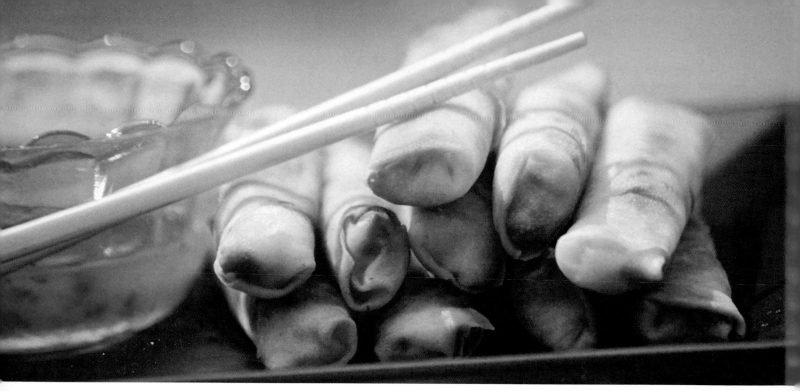

Spring Rolls

Shared by Nesia Baker, Clinton

1	pound ground pork	salt, to taste
2	carrot sticks, shredded	pepper, to taste
2	celery sticks, shredded	egg roll wrappers*
3-4	garlic cloves, minced	chili sauce, optional*
2	scallions, chopped	

Instructions:

In a large heavy skillet, brown ground pork over medium heat until cooked through. Add carrots, celery, garlic, scallions, salt and pepper and continue to cook until veggies soften. Place two-three tablespoons of pork mixture in each egg roll wrapper, roll until edges come together and bake in a 350 degree oven until crispy brown or pan fry. Serve with a bowl of chili sauce for dipping. To add spice to egg roll, mix in chili sauce to taste to egg roll filling. You can substitute pork with chicken, shrimp or beef.

* *Available at Asian markets.*

Guacamole

Shared by Diane Gardner, Madison

3	small tomatoes, diced	2	limes, juiced
4-5	ripe avocados, peeled and diced		red pepper flakes, to taste
$^1/_2$	small red onion, finely chopped		salt, to taste
			pepper, to taste
3	tablespoons sour cream	$^1/_2$	bunch fresh cilantro, chopped

Instructions:

Combine tomatoes, avocados, onion and sour cream, add lime to taste and mix in salt, pepper and red pepper flakes to taste. Add cilantro last. Serve immediately with cheesy crisps, tortilla chips or any Mexican dish.

Triopita–Greek Cheese Turnovers

Shared by Viki Kolyvas, Tidewater Inn, Madison

$1^1/_2$ pounds feta cheese, crumbled

1 pound Farmer's cheese

2 tablespoons parmesan cheese, grated

6 eggs, separated

1 pound fillo pastry sheets, 9 x 14 sheets

$^1/_2$ pound unsalted butter, melted

Instructions:

Advance Preparation: Wrap cheeses in cloth dish towels (not terry) and refrigerate overnight.

Filling: Crumble feta and Farmer's cheeses and mix together with parmesan cheese and egg yolks. Beat egg whites until stiff and dry. Fold egg whites into cheese mixture.

Assembly: Place a slightly dampened dish towel onto your work surface and cover this with waxed paper. Open fillo onto this waxed paper and cover with another piece of wax paper.

Place another piece of wax paper on your work surface. Take one piece of fillo out and with a pastry brush, butter a strip down the center few inches of the rectangle. At one end of the rectangle, place 2-3 tablespoons of the cheese filling. Fold in the sides of the fillo, lengthwise, to overlap slightly down the center.

Next, butter the length of the fillo and begin at the filling end and fold down the length as if you were folding an American flag in a triangle. Secure the end with a brush of melted butter and place it onto a parchment-lined or buttered baking sheet, seam side down. Repeat until all filling is used, makes approximately 48 pieces. Bake at 350 degrees for 20-30 minutes, until golden brown.

Variation: Spanakopita (Greek Spinach Turnovers)

In the filling process: Take 1/4 pound butter and 2–10 ounce packages fresh chopped spinach and heat together, add this to the cheese mixture and continue with directions.

Mel's Rueben Dip

Shared by Kim Castaldo, Madison

8 ounces cream cheese, softened and cut into pieces	1 cup Swiss cheese, grated
1/2 cup sour cream	2 teaspoons onion, finely chopped
1 cup sauerkraut, drained and chopped	1 tablespoon ketchup
1/2 pound lean corn beef, chopped fine	2 teaspoons spicy brown mustard

Instructions:

Combine all ingredients, put in a small oven proof casserole dish and bake at 375 degrees for 30 minutes covered, and for 5 more minutes uncovered. Serve with miniature rye bread hunks or crackers.

Gougeres Parsillacs–Cheese Puffs

Shared by Adam Calkins, Lyme

For the Pastry:

1	cup water
3	ounces unsalted butter, cut into pieces
1	teaspoon salt
1	cup all purpose flour

5   large eggs, blended, should total about 1 cup

$^1/_2$ cup gruyere, grated

$^1/_2$ cup comte, grated

Instructions:

Bring the water to a boil in a small heavy bottomed saucepan. Add the butter and season and stir until the butter is melted. Remove the pan from the heat, add all the flour at once and beat vigorously until the mixture is very smooth. Return the mixture to moderate heat and stir for an additional minute or so until the dough forms a ball.

Turn the dough into a bowl and stir for a short while until it has cooled slightly. Make a well into the center of the dough and add the egg mixture slowly, in four portions, blending very well between each addition.

Stir the cheese into the warm dough. Preheat oven to 425 degrees.

Forming the puffs:

Line 2 large baking sheets with parchment paper or silpat liners. Fill a pastry bag fitted with a $^1/_2$ inch opening and squeeze round hills of dough about 1 inch high onto the baking sheets, spacing them $1^1/_2$ inches apart. This makes roughly 30–36 puffs.

Glaze:

1 egg
1 teaspoon water
Pinch salt

Instructions:

Blend well and with a pastry brush lightly paint each blob. Bake in middle racks for 20 minutes and brown. Turn down oven to 400 degrees and bake for 10 more minutes or until the Gougeres feel crisp and very light.

Gougeres Parsillacs–Cheese Puffs *(continued)*

For the Garnish:

¹/₄ cup parmesan reggiano, grated

3 tablespoon parsley, very finely chopped

2 large garlic cloves, minced

1 fresh lemon, juiced

Instructions:

Mix all ingredients together and sprinkle over the warm Gougeres. Serve immediately.

Gougeres freeze well and can be reheated in a 400 degree oven for 10 minutes until warmed through.

*Cheese can be found at Fromage Fine Foods and Coffees in Old Saybrook or at your favorite cheese shop.

Portabello Mushrooms Stuffed with Spinach, Walnuts & Cheese

Shared by The Cooking Company, Killingworth

1¹/₂ cups minced onion

3 tablespoons olive oil

6 tablespoons walnuts, coarsely chopped

3 garlic cloves, minced

3 cups spinach, cooked, squeezed of excess water and chopped

¹/₂ cup feta cheese, crumbled

1 cup gruyere cheese, grated

3 tablespoons fresh dill, chopped

4 portabello mushrooms
   salt, to taste
   pepper, to taste

Instructions:

Remove the stems from the portabellos and chop them. In a skillet, cook the onion in the olive oil, stirring occasionally, until colored lightly. Add the chopped mushroom stems and cook a few minutes more. Add the walnuts and garlic and cook the mixture, stirring for 1 minute. Remove from the heat. Add the spinach, feta, gruyere, dill, salt and pepper.

Brush the mushroom caps with olive oil. Sprinkle with salt and pepper and roast in a 350 degree oven for 10–15 minutes or until the mushrooms begin to get soft but are not cooked all the way through.

When the mushroom caps are cool enough to handle, divide the spinach mixture among them, mounding it gently. (May be prepared ahead up to this point). Bake in a preheated 350 degree oven for 10 minutes (20–25 minutes if prepared ahead) or until the filling is heated through and the tops are lightly browned. Serves 4.

Cheese Wafers—
South Carolina Style

Shared by Loretta Tallevast, Lake City , South Carolina

This is the recipe for the cheese wafers that we served at our open houses and book signings from our first book. It was a sample of what was to come. So here it is! It's delicious and easy to make. This is my Mom's recipe from Lake City , South Carolina .

2¹/₂ cups plain flour
2 sticks butter, softened
8 ounces NY sharp cheddar cheese, grated

1 teaspoon red pepper
1 dash salt

Instructions:

Mix all ingredients together and form into a long roll. Refrigerate 1–2 hours. Cut into slices and bake at 350 degrees for about 10 minutes. This makes about 6 dozen small wafers.

Caviar Pie "Diane"

Shared by Diane Ifkovic, Guilford

*This is a favorite, easy to prepare and delicious. My husband and
I entertain extensively on the water and we always serve this.*

³/₄ cup sweet onion, minced	8 ounces cream cheese, softened
6 hard cooked eggs	²/₃ cup sour cream
3 tablespoons mayonnaise	6 ounces caviar

Instructions:

Drain onion on paper towels for 30 minutes. Lightly butter bottom and
sides of an 8 inch springform pan. Chop eggs, mix with mayonnaise and
spread in bottom of pan. Sprinkle with onions. Beat cream cheese and
sour cream together until smooth. Drop by tablespoons onto onion and
gently spread with back of spoon. Cover pan with plastic wrap and chill
overnight. Just before serving, gently spread caviar onto cream cheese
layer. Remove sides of pan and garnish with parsley sprigs. Serve with
party rye, toast or water crackers.

Cranberry Salsa Crackers

Shared by Diane Ifkovic, Guilford

1¹/₂ cups cranberries	2 tablespoons fresh cilantro, minced
2 green onions	1 tablespoon fresh ginger, grated
1 small jalapeno pepper, seeded and minced	8 ounces cream cheese
¹/₄ cup sugar	sesame melba rounds
1 teaspoon lemon juice	

Instructions:

Position knife blade in food processor. Add cranberries and pulse until
finely chopped. Transfer to a bowl and stir in green onions and next
5 ingredients. Cover and refrigerate for 4 hours. To serve, spread 1 tablespoon of cream cheese on each melba toast and top with one teaspoon of
cranberry mixture and garnish with cilantro leaves.

Oven Barbecued Chicken Bites

Shared by Jan Hunter, Madison

Instructions:

In a large bowl, combine water, chicken, soy sauce and salt. Cover and refrigerate overnight. Pre-heat oven to 350 degrees. Drain the chicken and place in a rimmed baking sheet and bake for 30 minutes.

In a heavy saucepan over medium high heat, combine barbecue sauce, root beer and ginger and simmer for 5 minutes. Remove chicken from oven, drain sauce and coat with $2/3$ of simmering barbeque sauce. Return to oven for another 15 minutes. Remove from oven and coat with remaining sauce prior to serving. Optional, top with sesame seeds, parsley and crushed red pepper.

8	cups water
3	pounds boneless chicken breast, cut in strips
$3/4$	cup soy sauce
$1/4$	cup salt
2	cups prepared barbecue sauce
$1/3$	cup root beer
$1/4$	cup ginger, peeled and minced

Nana's Seafood Salad

Shared by Phyllis Carroll, Cape Cod

1 pound shrimp, peeled

1 pound sea scallops

4-5 lemon slices

2 teaspoons cilantro, chopped
romaine lettuce, shredded

2 ripe mangoes, diced

1/2 small red onion, diced

2 teaspoons ginger, finely chopped

1 teaspoon garlic, chopped and sautéed in a small bit of olive oil

Instructions:

Gently poach shrimp and scallops in water with lemon slices and cilantro. Do not overcook, 2–3 minutes for scallops and until the shrimp turn light pink. You can do separately if you like. Refrigerate until chilled. Slice scallops in half and add the remaining ingredients and gently toss with the following marinade.

Marinade:

4 teaspoons sweet hot chili sauce or regular chili sauce with a little honey

2 limes, juiced

4 tablespoons vegetable oil

1 teaspoon ground cumin
salt, to taste
pepper, to taste
cilantro, chopped

Instructions:

Mix together and toss with the shrimp and scallop mixture.

Serve in chilled, stemless wine glasses whose rims have been moistened with a lime and then dipped into coarse sea salt. Line the bottom of the glasses with lettuce then add seafood mixture. Garnish with a tortilla chip or make melon balls to look like olives, thread balls on a toothpick and place on top of seafood salad.

Breakfast, Brunch & Breads

Nantucket French Toast

Cheddar Cheese Biscuits

Lobster Eggs Benedict

Southern Breakfast Casserole

Red Lentil Quiche with Goat Cheese

Creme Brulee French Toast

French Frittata

Blueberry Stuffed French Toast

Captain's Cheesebake

Braeden's Christmas Oatmeal

Pop's Waffles

Breakfast Pie

Popovers

Mexican Cornbread

Zucchini Muffins

Bee and Thistle Inn Granola

Christmas Coffee Cake

Grandpa Wilson's Pumpkin Bread

Fruit Scones

Cheese Bread

Keek's Banana Bread

The Lily Pad's Banana Bread

Denison House Pancakes

Tomato Bacon Quiche

breakfast, brunch & breads

Nantucket French Toast

Shared by Chef Robert Crimm, S-CAR-GO, Old Lyme

I got this recipe from a dear friend and a wonderful chef, Annie Haviland. When the wind is blowing off the water of the Connecticut shoreline there is no better way to wake the family than with the aromas of fresh ground organic coffee brewing, the inviting aromas of warming maple syrup and the Nantucket French toast on the stove. They will come running. Try doing most of the prep the night before, that way your morning will be relaxed!

1 cup real Maple syrup	dash nutmeg
dried fruit, sliced apricots and cranberries work well	thick bread, rustic and hardy
nuts, walnuts or pecans	1-2 slices ham, may substitute turkey
4 eggs	1-2 slices good Swiss or Cheddar cheese
1/4 cup heavy cream	1 tablespoon butter
dash cinnamon	

Instructions:

Mix real maple syrup (do not skimp on the syrup, it makes all the difference in the world) dried fruit and nuts in a small saucepan, put on stove top and warm on low heat.

Mix eggs, heavy cream, cinnamon and nutmeg in a large bowl and set aside. Take bread and cut into 2 inch thick slices. Next, take the slices and cut in the middle, but not all the way through, as to make a pocket. When all the bread has been cut, you will want to take a slice or two of ham and cheese and stuff it into the pockets. It is ok if the ham and cheese hang out a bit.

Once all the bread is stuffed, take a skillet and melt a tablespoon of butter on medium high. Dip the stuffed bread into the reserve egg mixture; let it soak a bit to get it wet. Then in the pan it goes. Put as many as your pan will fit without touching. You will want to let them be for at least 5 minutes a side. They are thick and need time to cook. Flip and let cook another 5 minutes. French toast can be warmed in a 250 degree oven while preparing other pieces.

Serve in the center of a large dinner plate with a spoon or two of the warm maple syrup. Be sure to get some of the dried fruit and nuts!

Cheddar Cheese Biscuits

Shared by Diane Gardner, Madison

2	cups Bisquick	1	8 ounce container sour cream
1/2	cup butter, softened	1/2	cup cheddar cheese, grated

Instructions:

Mix all ingredients together. Form into small mounds and place on greased cookie sheet. Flatten each biscuits with fingers. Bake at 450 degrees for 10–12 minutes. Serve warm or at room temperature, these are fantastic with a little honey drizzled over them. If you have left over biscuits, the next morning, slice and toast in the oven with butter and serve with jam.

Lobster Eggs Benedict

Shared by James Martell, sous chef for the Flood Tide Restaurant located at the Inn at Mystic, Mystic

4	ounces simmered butter	1/2	teaspoon parsley, diced
2	1 ounce lobster claws, picked	1	English muffin, cut in half and toasted
1	ounce lobster claw and knuckle, picked		pinch of cayenne pepper
2	egg yolks		salt, to taste
3	tablespoons white wine		pepper, to taste
1/2	teaspoon lemon juice	2	eggs, poached
2	drops water	2	slices Canadian bacon

Instructions:

In a small sauté pan, heat butter and lobster meat until butter becomes rosie pink. Strain lobster and cool. Reserve both lobster and butter separately. In a medium mixing bowl, combine egg yolks, wine, lemon juice, water and parsley with a balloon whisk. Place the bowl over a pan of hot water, continue whisking and gradually add the reserved butter. The sauce should thicken. Place both sides of toasted English muffin on a plate and top with Canadian bacon, poached egg and reserved lobster. Spoon prepared sauce over the top and serve warm.

Southern Breakfast Casserole

Shared by Loretta Tallevast, Lake City, South Carolina

This is a great holiday recipe that I make for my family on Thanksgiving morning and Christmas. It's delicious and easy to prepare ahead so you have more time in the morning to spend with family.

1 pound sharp cheddar cheese, grated	2 cups milk
1 pound bacon, cooked and diced in small pieces	1 teaspoon dry mustard
7 slices white bread, crust cut off and cubed	7 eggs, well beaten
	salt, to taste
	pepper, to taste

Instructions:

Pat bacon to remove all the excess fat. Mix together all ingredients and pour into a greased 9 x 13 inch baking dish. Refrigerate overnight. Bake at 350 degrees for 45 minutes. You can use sausage or ham instead of bacon.

Red Lentil Quiche with Goat Cheese

Shared by Monica Pitney, East Haddam

Being a part of the staff at Fromage in Old Saybrook, I love to incorporate the wide variety of cheeses that are available daily. This is a wonderful crustless quiche that uses goat cheese which is lower in calories than many other cheeses. The red lentils are so pretty and fresh goat cheese is available year round.

1/2 cup red lentils	1 cup milk
1/2 cup roasted tomatoes, chopped	2 teaspoons Italian seasoning
4 eggs, beaten	4 ounces goat cheese
	1 cup onion, chopped

Instructions:

Preheat oven to 375 degrees. In a saucepan, cook lentils in boiling water for 20 minutes, then drain. In a large bowl, combine lentils with all remaining ingredients. Pour into a pie plate and bake for 45 minutes. Let sit for 10 minutes before slicing.

Creme Brulee French Toast

Shared by Lee White, Old Lyme

✳

1	cup pecans, chopped (optional)	5	eggs
1	stick unsalted butter	1¹/₂	cups half and half
1	cup brown sugar	¹/₄	teaspoon salt
2	tablespoons light or dark corn syrup	1	tablespoon Cointreau or Grand Marnier (optional)
	French bread, crusts removed and sliced into ³/₄ inch thick slabs		

Instructions:

Butter a 13 x 9 inch glass pan, or spray with cooking oil. Spread chopped pecans in bottom of pan. Melt together butter, brown sugar and corn syrup and pour evenly over pecans. Fit slabs of bread tightly over butter-sugar mixture. Beat eggs, half and half, vanilla, salt and liqueur and pour over bread slices. Cover and chill for at least 8 hours or overnight. Bake in preheated 350 degree oven for 35–40 minutes. Serve immediately with chocolate dipped strawberries. This will serve 6 to 8.

Chocolate-dipped Strawberries

Rinse and dry about 1 pound stemmed strawberries. In a small pot, slowly melt 8-ounces of good chocolate chips. When the chocolate chips are melted (do not boil them), place waxed paper or parchment on a baking dish on the counter. Holding the strawberries by the stem with one hand and, with the other, dipped the pot of chocolate to the side, cover about half of each strawberry. Place on paper and chill for at least 4 hours or a day or more.

French Frittata

Shared by 3 Liberty Green, Clinton

12	fresh asparagus spears	2	tablespoons extra virgin olive oil
12	large eggs	1	medium Vidalia onion, chopped fine
1	cup milk (any kind but skim)	1	large leek, white part only, thinly sliced
2	tablespoons Grey Poupon mustard	$1^1/_4$	cups Swiss cheese, shredded
1	teaspoon salt		
$^1/_2$	teaspoon pepper		

Instructions:

Thoroughly wash asparagus and cut 1 inch off the bottom of each, discard these ends. Take 6 of the asparagus and cut into 3 inch pieces, blanch in boiling water, drain and set aside as they will be used for the decorative presentation. Chop the remaining 6 asparagus spears into small pieces, blanch in boiling water, drain and set aside. In a medium sized bowl, combine eggs, milk, mustard and salt and pepper. Whisk thoroughly to blend. In a 10 inch oven proof skillet, heat olive oil over medium heat, sauté onion until lightly browned, add asparagus and leeks and continue to cook for another minute. Keep heat on medium and add egg mixture and 1 cup of cheese, with a spatula, gently move mixture back and forth to combine. Remove skillet from heat, and decoratively place the 3 inch pieces of asparagus on top. Place the skillet back on burner, sprinkle with remaining cheese and let cook for 1 minute. Place skillet under broiler for 3–5 minutes, until lightly browned. Let frittata rest for a few minutes before slicing and serve with crusty loaf of Rye bread.

Blueberry Stuffed French Toast

Shared by Another Second Penny Inn, Stonington

8-10	slices firm bread	1	tablespoon cornstarch
4	ounces soft cream cheese	$^1/_2$	cup water
$^1/_2$	pint blueberries, fresh	$^1/_2$	tablespoon butter or margarine
$1^1/_2$	cups milk		
2	eggs	1-2	ounces maple syrup
$^3/_4$	cup sugar (divided)	$^1/_2$	teaspoon vanilla
$^1/_4$	teaspoon nutmeg		

Instructions:

Prepare 6 four inch springform pans by lining them with parchment paper. Cut crusts off bread and trim each slice to fit the bottom of each pan. Spread slice of bread with as much or as little cream cheese as desired and place in pan. Sprinkle with half the blueberries using more or less as desired. Cut the remaining bread into cubes (removing crusts) and place on top of the blueberries. Combine milk, eggs, maple syrup, vanilla and $^1/_8$ cup of sugar in a bowl, whisk until well blended. Use a $^1/_4$ cup to measure and divide, then pour mixture evenly between the 6 pans. Cover and refrigerate overnight.

In the morning, preheat oven to 350 degrees. Mix nutmeg and $^1/_8$ cup sugar together and sprinkle over the bread cubes. Cover lightly with foil and bake for 30 minutes. Remove foil and bake until golden and inserted knife comes out clean, about 15 minutes. Meanwhile in a small sauce pan mix cornstarch, $^1/_2$ cup water and remaining sugar. Bring to a boil over medium heat, stirring occasionally and cook until thickened. Add remaining blueberries and butter and simmer until sauce is to your liking. Strawberries can be substituted for blueberries.

This recipe serves 6.

Captain's Cheesebake

Shared by Mary and Jim Brewster, Owners,
Captain Stannard Inn, Westbrook

This is a versatile and hardy meal for any time of the day. We have served it to our family and friends on special occasions for many years and it always brings us joyful memories when we serve it to our guests. We have served it with fruit at breakfast, with salad and crusty rolls for brunch, and as a late night dinner after a show. Our guests love it!

12 slices Pepperidge Farm bread, cubed

$1/2$ pound sharp Cheddar cheese, shredded

2 cups milk

3 eggs, beaten

$1/4$ teaspoon pepper

$1^1/2$ teaspoon dry English mustard

$1/2$ teaspoon salt

12 Jone's breakfast sausage, cooked and sliced in $1/2''$ pieces

1 can Campbell's cream of mushroom soup

paprika, to taste

Instructions:

Grease 11″ x 13″ Pyrex dish. Line the bottom with bread cubes. Sprinkle the cheese over the top. In a medium sized bowl, combine the milk, eggs, mustard, salt and pepper and pour over the top. Spread the cooked sausage over egg mixture. Spoon the can of soup over this. Sprinkle with paprika and bake at 350 degrees for 30 minutes covered and then 30 more minutes uncovered.

Substitutions can be made by using wheat bread instead of white, but keep it soft. And light sausage in place of regular sausage.

Best of all, it is wonderful made a day ahead and it can be frozen.

Braeden's Christmas Oatmeal

Shared by Tania Kosiewicz, Madison

This is especially yummy after opening presents on Christmas morning. I make it the day before and refrigerate. Then when presents are being opened, I pop it in the oven. Everyone loves it!

1/2	cup butter	1	teaspoon vanilla
2	eggs, beaten	1	teaspoon cinnamon
1	cup sugar	1/2	teaspoon nutmeg
1/4	cup oil	1	teaspoon salt
2	teaspoons baking powder	3	cups oatmeal, Quick or Old Fashioned
1	cup milk		

Instructions:

Mix butter, eggs, sugar, oil, baking powder, milk, vanilla, cinnamon, nutmeg and salt until well blended in a large mixing bowl. Stir in oatmeal until combined. Spray baking dish with cooking spray and add oatmeal mixture. Bake at 350 degrees for 45 minutes or until done.

Serve with a lot of butter and brown sugar on top and hot milk poured over it.

Pop's Waffles

Shared by Liz Crowther, Madison

The last of the family's secret recipe's! I can't make enough of these for my grandchildren! Enjoy!

2	cups flour	4	eggs, separated
4	teaspoons baking powder	2	cups milk
1	teaspoon salt	1	stick butter, melted

Instructions:

Whisk dry ingredients together. In a separate bowl, mix together milk with beaten egg yolks. Whisk dry ingredients into egg mixture. Add melted butter and stir. Beat egg whites until stiff and gently fold into batter. Pour into preheated waffle iron. Serve with warm maple syrup or your favorite topping. This makes 3 large waffles.

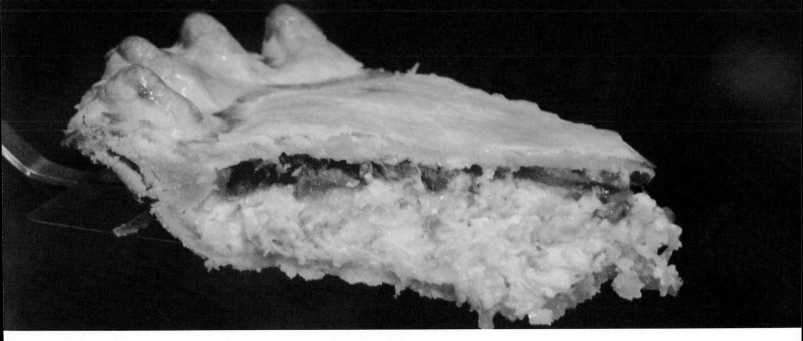

Breakfast Pie

Shared by 3 Liberty Green, Clinton

2	prepared pie crusts	$^1/_4$	teaspoon salt
2$^1/_2$	cups Cheddar cheese, shredded	$^1/_4$	teaspoon pepper
2	tablespoons Vidalia onion, diced	2	eggs, beaten lightly
		$^2/_3$	cup milk or half and half
1	large tomato, sliced thin	1	egg, beaten lightly

Instructions:

Place one pie crust in a 9 inch pie plate. Cover with the cheese and evenly distribute onion over cheese. Spread tomato slices over the onion and sprinkle with salt and pepper. Combine eggs with milk or half and half and pour over the tomatoes. Place the second pie crust on top and tuck the top crust under the bottom edge to seal. Brush edges and top of crust with beaten egg. Make four 1 inch slits in top of crust so that the steam can be released. Bake for 45 minutes in a 350 degree oven. Remove and allow to sit for a few minutes before slicing. This can be prepared the night before, refrigerated and covered.

Popovers

Shared by Shari Lariviere, Madison

These light airy puffs of goodness hot out of the oven make my mouth water just thinking about them. Also known as Yorkshire pudding, popovers are traditionally served with prime rib. However, as far back as I can remember they have always been a special family breakfast for us. My mom is the popover master and I have been working to recreate the perfection; a crisp outside and a soft, luscious inside 4 or 5 times its original size.

1	cup flour	$^1/_2$	teaspoon salt
1	cup skim milk	2	eggs (can substitute egg
1	teaspoon olive oil		beaters)

Instructions:

Combine all ingredients except the eggs and whisk until completely mixed, about 2 minutes. Gently mix in the eggs. Pour batter into well greased custard cups, about $^2/_3$ full. Bake for 45 minutes in a 400 degree oven. Be sure to place the oven rack towards the bottom of the oven as they rise substantially.

Mexican Cornbread

Shared by Jean Johnson, Guilford

This recipe quickly became a family favorite on our annual skiing trips in Aspen and Vail. It can be served any time of the day, for breakfast or as a side to pork tenderloin or chili.

1	box Jiffy cornbread mix	2	cans green chilis, sliced
1/2	cup canola oil	2	cans Jalapeno peppers, sliced
1	cup sour cream	1	8-ounce package cheddar cheese, grated
1	can cream style corn		
1	egg, beaten		

Instructions:

Mix first 5 ingredients together. Spread half of this mixture into a greased 8 inch square baking dish. Spread peppers over that and sprinkle half of cheese over peppers. Top with the remaining cornbread mixture and finish with the cheese. Bake at 325 degrees for 1 hour.

Zucchini Muffins

Shared by Anne Marie Marchitto, The Waiting Station, Branford

2	cups all purpose flour	1/4	cup vegetable oil
3	teaspoons baking powder	3/4	cup fresh zucchini, grated
1/2	teaspoon salt	1/2	cup carrots, grated
1/2	cup white sugar	1/2	cup walnuts, chopped
1	egg, beaten	1/2	cup raisins, softened
3/4	cup milk		

Instructions:

Preheat oven to 400 degrees. In a large bowl, stir together the flour, baking powder, salt and sugar. Make a well in the center. In a small bowl beat egg, milk and oil together. Pour all at once into the well of the flour mixture. Mix quickly and lightly until moistened, do not beat. The batter will be lumpy. Fold in remaining ingredients. Pour the batter into prepared muffin pans and bake at 400 degrees for 25 minutes or until golden brown.

Bee and Thistle Inn Granola

Shared by The Bee and Thistle Inn, Old Lyme

2	sticks butter, unsalted	1	teaspoon cinnamon
1	cup light brown sugar	2	cups oats
3	tablespoons honey	¹/₂	cup almonds, sliced
¹/₂	cup Puffed Rice cereal	¹/₂	cup dried apricots, diced

Instructions:

Preheat oven to 375°

In a saucepan, over low heat, melt butter, sugar and honey together until slightly frothy. In a separate mixing bowl, combine the remaining ingredients. Be sure not to touch this sugar mixture (very hot). Stir sugar mixture into the granola mixture until evenly mixed. Coat a rimmed sheet pan with vegetable oil or butter. Bake mixture until golden brown, stirring occasionally. Depending on oven, cook about 12–15 minutes. Allow to cool, break into desired size pieces. You can store about 10 days in an airtight container. You may substitute any dried fruit of your choice.

Christmas Coffee Cake

Shared by Monica Pitney, East Haddam

**This cake works great any time of the day because it is not "too sweet".
The crème fraiche adds the right amount of richness.**

1 cup sugar	pinch of salt
2 eggs	1 cup crème fraiche
1 teaspoon vanilla	
1/4 pound butter	**Topping:**
2 cups flour	1/4 cup sugar
1 teaspoon baking soda	3/4 cup crushed nuts
1 teaspoon baking powder	1 teaspoon cinnamon

Instructions:

Combine 3 ingredients to form topping.

Preheat oven to 350 degrees. In a large bowl, completely combine sugar, eggs, vanilla and butter. Add in dry ingredients and then add the crème fraiche. Pour 1/2 of this batter into a greased bundt pan. Pour 1/2 of the topping on top and then pour the remaining 1/2 of the batter on top of the topping. Finally, sprinkle remaining 1/2 of topping and bake for 30–35 minutes. This is especially tasty served with a nice dark roasted cup of coffee!

Grandpa Wilson's Pumpkin Bread

Shared by Liz Crowther, Madison

$3^1/_2$	cups flour	3	cups sugar
2	teaspoons baking soda	$^2/_3$	cup water
$1^1/_2$	teaspoons salt	1	cup vegetable oil
1	teaspoon cinnamon	2	cups canned pumpkin
1	teaspoon nutmeg		nuts, optional
4	eggs		

Instructions:

Sift together first 5 ingredients and set aside. Beat eggs, one at a time and add sugar, water, oil and pumpkin. Combine dry ingredients with wet and mix. Bake in 3 greased and floured loaf pans filled half way. Bake at 350 degrees for 1 hour or until toothpick inserted into center comes out clean. Slice and enjoy!

Fruit Scones

Shared by Mystic Market East, Mystic

$2^{1}/_{4}$ cups flour	$1^{1}/_{8}$ cups dried fruit (crystallized
$^{1}/_{8}$ cup baking powder	ginger, cherries, apricots etc.)
pinch salt	$19^{1}/_{4}$ ounces heavy cream
$^{1}/_{2}$ cup sugar	$^{1}/_{4}$ cup coarse sanding sugar

Instructions:

Mix all dry ingredients in a Kitchen Aid with a paddle. When combined, add all fruit of your choice. Pour cream in slowly while mixer is still running. Remove batter from bowl and press into a large circular shape approximately 10 inches in diameter and $1^{1}/_{2}$ inches thick. Cut into 10 wedges and place on a cookie sheet lined with parchment paper and sprayed with cooking spray. Sprinkle coarse sanding sugar on top of scones and bake for 20–25 minutes in a 350 degree oven. Rotate pan inside oven every 5 minutes. Scones are done when they are firm to touch and light golden brown in color.

Cheese Bread

Shared by Ann Rowley, Old Saybrook

1 stick butter, unsalted	$^{1}/_{4}$ cup Parmigiano-Reggiano
2 tablespoons extra virgin olive oil	cheese, grated
$^{1}/_{2}$ pound Roquefort cheese	$^{1}/_{2}$ teaspoon garlic, minced
	1 French baguette sliced thin

Instructions:

Combine butter, oil and cheeses in a small saucepan. Add garlic and stir over low heat for about 5 minutes. Brush butter mixture onto bread slices and bake on a cookie sheet for 3–5 minutes in a 500 degree oven. Cheese bread should be golden brown and served warm.

Keek's Banana Bread

Shared by Carol J. Newton, Madison

*Whenever I make this my family asks me to make
2 loaves because it gets eaten so quickly!*

1	cup sugar	1	teaspoon baking soda
$1/3$	cup butter, softened	$1/2$	teaspoon salt
2	eggs	$1/4$	teaspoon baking powder
$1/3$	cup water	$1^1/2$	cups bananas (3-4)
$1^2/3$	cups flour		

Instructions:

Preheat oven to 350 degrees. Grease bottom only of loaf pan. Mix sugar and butter together. Blend in eggs and add water. Stir in remaining ingredients except for bananas.

Smoosh bananas into large chunks with clean hands and add to mixture. Fold in bananas and then pour into pan and bake for 55–60 minutes.

The Lily Pad's Banana Bread

Shared by The Lily Pad, Milford

Our guests love this banana bread!

2-3	bananas, very ripe and mashed	$1/2$	teaspoon salt
2	eggs, well beaten	$1/4$	teaspoon baking soda
$2/3$	cup sugar	2	teaspoons baking powder
$1/3$	cup butter	$1^3/4$	cups flour
		$1/2$	cup raisins

Instructions:

In a mixer, combine bananas, eggs, sugar and butter and beat very well. Add salt, baking soda, baking powder and flour and blend until smooth. Pour banana mixture into greased 9 x 5 x 3 inch loaf pan and bake for approximately one hour in a 350 degree oven. Cool and remove from pan, serve with cream cheese, jam or butter.

Denison House Pancakes

Shared by Jim and Sandra Wright, Stonington

2 cups flour
2 teaspoons baking powder
$^1/_2$ teaspoon salt
1 tablespoon powdered sugar
2 eggs, well beaten
$1^3/_4$ cups milk
1 teaspoon vanilla

Our home was built in 1710 by Edward Denison, and these pancakes are named for him.

Instructions:

In a bowl, combine all dry ingredients. In a separate bowl, combine eggs, milk and vanilla, beat with a hand whisk until color is uniform. Add flour mixture and whisk until smooth. More milk may be necessary to thin the batter, especially if it sits for more than a few minutes.

Heat a nonstick fry pan or griddle over medium heat and drop batter by $^1/_4$ cupfuls onto pan. Turn when bubbles cover the surface and bottom is golden brown. Remove from pan when pancake is golden on both sides. Pancakes are light and tasty and best served warm with your favorite butter and syrup.

This recipe makes about a dozen pancakes.

Tomato Bacon Quiche

Shared by Zandra Baker, Palmer's Market, Darien

1	10-inch prepared pie shell	2	cups cheddar cheese, shredded
4	plum tomatoes, diced	6	eggs
$^1/_4$	cup olive oil	1	quart heavy cream
1	tablespoon sage		salt, to taste
1	tablespoon rosemary		pepper, to taste
6	strips of bacon, cooked crispy		

Instructions:

Place pie shell on sheet pan and bake empty for 5–10 minutes until just golden brown. In a small skillet, sauté tomatoes in olive oil with sage and rosemary. Place this mixture in a bowl to cool. Add bacon and cheddar cheese to tomato mixture and combine. Place this whole mixture in the center of the pie shell in a tall mound. In a medium bowl, mix together the eggs and heavy cream. Pour this egg/cream mixture over the mound to fill the pie shell. Place in a 350 degree oven for 12–15 minutes. Let set for 10 minutes prior to serving.

simmering SOUPS, STEWS & CHILIS

FRENCH ONION SOUP

STU'S OYSTER STEW

WINTER WHITE BEAN CHILI

ROASTED WINTER VEGETABLE BISQUE

CREAM OF POTATO NOODLE SOUP

BUTTERNUT SQUASH AND APPLE SOUP

AUNT KELLEY'S CHICKEN SOUP

CREAMY CRAB SOUP

DENNISON ROAD CHOWDER

TURKEY & VEGETABLE CHILI

WINTER CHILI

CREAMY HAM AND POTATO SOUP

ARTICHOKE BLUE-CHEESE BISQUE

PUMPKIN BISQUE

CINCINNATI CHILI

ASPARAGUS AND CRAB MEAT SOUP

HUNGARIAN MUSHROOM SOUP

CHICKEN AND PAPPARDELLE SOUP

MISSISSIPPI 5 HOUR STEW

LIZ'S SWEET AND SPICY CHILI

BARBARA BARKER'S CHILI

CHILI CON CARNE

HEARTY BEEF BARLEY SOUP

HEARTY BEEF VEGETABLE SOUP

NEW ENGLAND CLAM CHOWDER

soups, stews & chilis

French Onion Soup

Shared by Shari Lariviere, Madison

Ahhhh, layers of hot soup, a crouton and melted cheese, a comfort food at its finest! The great thing about making soup is that there really is no precise science to it. We always laugh in my family when I make a good soup because I always say "glad you enjoyed it, you'll never have it again", simply because I love to cook and hardly ever follow a recipe, not even my own!

2	tablespoons butter	1	can beef consomme
2	tablespoons olive oil	2	tablespoons brandy
5	large onions, sliced		
1/2	teaspoon sugar		**Croutons:**
2	tablespoons flour		day old loaf of bread
1/2	cup vermouth, dry		crushed garlic
1	49-ounce can of beef stock or 5 cups homemade beef stock		olive oil
		4	thick slices gruyere cheese

Instructions:

Slice bread and spread with crushed garlic and drizzle with olive oil. Bake for 20 minutes in a 250 degree oven until crispy.

In a large pot, sauté onions in butter and olive oil for about 20–30 minutes. Add sugar, flour and vermouth. Continue to cook onion mixture for another 20 minutes. Add beef stock and consumé and cook for another 20 minutes. Add brandy and cook for 10 more minutes, ladle soup into oven proof bowls. Top with crouton and a slice of gruyere cheese. Place under broiler and broil until cheese is bubbly.

Stu's Oyster Stew

Shared by Stuart London, executive chef
for Sankow's Beaver Brook Farm, Lyme

I created this recipe when I was executive chef at the Old Lyme Inn for their Christmas menu. I've been told by my food writer friend, Lee White, that this is "the best and most sensuous oyster stew I've ever had".

1	quart heavy cream	1/2	teaspoon fresh black pepper, ground
32	oysters, shucked with juices, set juices aside	4	tablespoons butter, unsalted
2	tablespoons Worcestershire sauce	4	slices dense toasted bread, crusts removed
1	tablespoon hot sauce		salt, to taste
1/2	teaspoon fresh nutmeg, grated		

Instructions:

In a heavy 3 or 4 quart pot on medium heat, reduce cream, oyster juice, Worcestershire sauce and hot sauce by about 1/3. Add nutmeg, pepper, oysters and butter. Stir and simmer until butter is incorporated and the oysters are lightly cooked, about 2 minutes. Taste to adjust seasonings. Place 1 piece of toasted bread in the bottom of 4 warm bowls. Pour stew over toasts.

Winter White Bean Chili

Shared by Phyllis Carroll, Cape Cod and Carolyn Sperry, Nantucket

4	boneless chicken breasts
2	tablespoons olive oil
1	cup onion, chopped
1	tablespoon cumin
1	teaspoon oregano
2	cups chicken broth
1	cup water
1	teaspoon lemon pepper
3	11-ounce cans white corn (undrained)
3	15-ounce cans white northern beans (undrained)
2	4-ounce cans green chilies, chopped
4	tablespoons lemon juice
	salt, to taste
	pepper, to taste
	1 tablespoon cilantro, chopped
¹/₂	cup monterey jack cheese, shredded

Instructions:

Wrap chicken in foil and bake for one hour in a 400 degree oven. Remove from oven and shred the chicken into small pieces. In a large dutch oven, heat olive oil and cook onion until just lightly browned. Add chicken and all remaining ingredients. Cook for 1 hour on low heat. Top with fresh cilantro and cheese.

When living in Colorado, attending the Air Force football games was so much fun. This chili was great for tailgating—hearty and delicious. It warmed our nearly frozen fingers and toes!

Roasted Winter Vegetable Bisque

Shared by Chef Robert Crimm, S-CAR-GO, Old Lyme

I make a lot of this and freeze it for those cold rainy days. It is great with a grilled ham and cheese sandwich. This is what the kids will say when they grow up "That is just like mom used to make." I think we all have one or two of those!

3	carrots, roughly chopped		olive oil, for coating veggies
8	sweet potatoes, roughly chopped		salt, to taste
			pepper, to taste
2	acorn squash, roughly chopped	2	gallons chicken stock
1	large white onion, chopped	1/2	tablespoon nutmeg

Instructions:

Peel and roughly chop carrots, sweet potatoes, acorn squash and onion. Put in a bowl and toss with olive oil, salt and pepper. Roast vegetables at 400 degrees on a cookie sheet for 30 to 40 minutes or until golden brown.

While roasting the vegetables, bring chicken stock and nutmeg to a boil. When vegetables are roasted, add to the stock boiling on the stove and continue to boil for 30 minutes. Run a stick blender through this bisque until smooth and serve. I like this with a slice of toasted rustic bread.

Cream of Potato Noodle Soup

Shared by Anne Marie Marchitto, The Waiting Station, Branford

In 1923 my mother was working as a Nanny in France and she told me that she would make this soup for the family she was caring for. She brought this recipe here to the United States and made this soup for her own family and passed it on to me.

1 gallon cold water	1/2 quart milk
1 teaspoon salt	1/2 stick butter
10 medium red potatoes, diced in 1/2 inch pieces	white pepper, to taste
1 pound wide egg noodles	1/2 teaspoon garlic salt
1 quart heavy cream	1/2 teaspoon onion salt

Instructions:

In a large soup pot, bring water, salt and potatoes to a boil and cook until the potatoes are just done. Add the egg noodles into the pot with potatoes and water and cook until al dente. Drain off some of the cooking liquid, but leave enough to cover the potatoes and noodles. Add the cream, milk, butter, and seasonings and simmer for 30 minutes in a double broiler pot. If the soup is too thick, add more milk.

Butternut Squash and Apple Soup

Shared by Garelick and Herbs, Greenwich, Westport and New Canaan

¹/₂ cup white onions, diced	¹/₄ cup maple syrup
2 tablespoons olive oil	3 quarts water
4 cups butternut squash, cubed	pinch of salt
1 cup applesauce	¹/₂ teaspoon cinnamon
¹/₂ cup brown sugar	

Instructions:

In a large heavy pot, sauté onion in olive oil on medium heat. Add butternut squash and cook until squash is beginning to soften. Add applesauce, stir in brown sugar and maple syrup, then add water and salt. Bring to a boil and continue boiling until squash is soft, when squash is cooked completely, remove from heat and put through a food processor to puree. This soup can be served hot or cold, dust the top with cinnamon prior to serving.

Aunt Kelley's Chicken Soup

Shared by Kelley McMahon, Hopedale, MA

Whenever I come to Madison to visit my sister and her family the first thing my nephew, Connor, says when I walk in the door is…"Aunt Kelley did you bring your chicken soup?"

Broth:

1	large chicken roaster
	water
1	whole bunch celery, chopped
$^1/_2$	teaspoon basil
$^1/_2$	teaspoon oregano
$^1/_2$	teaspoon thyme
1	bag baby carrots, chopped

Finish:

1	large Spanish onion, chopped
$^1/_2$	teaspoon basil
$^1/_2$	teaspoon oregano
$^1/_2$	teaspoon thyme
1	teaspoon salt
$^1/_2$	teaspoon pepper
1	pound pasta

Instructions:

Cook oven roaster until timer pops out or until cooked through. Remove meat from roaster, cut into chunks and put aside. In a large pot, place all chicken bones plus wings, skin, etc. Fill the pot with enough water to cover the chicken bones. Add the leaves only of the celery, basil, oregano and thyme. Bring to a boil and then continue cooking on medium heat for 2 hours. Add more water as it cooks down. Drain bones and celery leaves from chicken stock and place stock in refrigerator for 1 hour. Skim fat off broth and place broth back on stove. Add carrots, onion, basil, oregano, thyme, salt and pepper and the cut up chicken pieces. Cook for 45 minutes on medium heat, then add pasta. Allow this to cook through for another 10 minutes or so.

Creamy Crab Soup

Shared by Ginger Carver, Madison

6	tablespoons butter	12	ounces crabmeat, cooked (about 1½ cups)
2½	cups fresh mushrooms, sliced (about 8-ounces)	¾	cup parmesan cheese, freshly grated
3	tablespoons flour	¼	cup good quality dry sherry
3	cups homemade chicken stock (may substitute canned chicken broth), low sodium		salt, to taste pepper, to taste
1½	cups heavy cream	½	cup fresh parsley, chopped

Instructions:

Melt 3 tablespoons butter in 10 inch skillet over medium heat. Add mushrooms and cook about 5 minutes, stirring occasionally until soft. Remove from heat, set aside.

Melt remaining 3 tablespoons butter in heavy 3 quart saucepan over medium heat, stir in flour until blended and smooth. Pour in chicken stock and cream, stirring constantly.

Cook and stir 8–10 minutes until chicken stock mixture thickens and just begins to boil. Add crabmeat and reserved mushrooms. Cook and stir 2–3 minutes longer until completely heated. Top with parsley prior to serving.

Dennison Road Chowder

Shared by Jahn Weingardt, Essex

*Inspired by the traditional Rhode Island style clam chowders, a simple
broth based meal carried by the local Portuguese fishermen in their
coffee thermoses. Dennison road was the original route that carried
fishermen and commerce travelers from the Essex shipyards
to New Haven, along the river, on horse drawn carts.*

1	tablespoon virgin olive oil	1/2	cup chicken stock
1	small clove garlic, chopped		salt, to taste
4	thick slices smoked bacon (best to get it from Cliff's in Essex)		pepper, to taste
1/2	cup local fingerling potatoes, chopped	2	dozen littleneck or cherry-stone clams, shucked in their own juices (Old Lyme Seafood has great clams)
1/2	cup leeks, chopped	1	tablespoon chives, fresh
1/2	cup clam juice, fresh	1	lemon

Instructions:

In a large heavy skillet over medium heat, warm olive oil, combine and
sauté garlic, bacon, potatoes and leeks until tender. Add clam juice and
chicken stock, season with salt and pepper. Add clams and cook on low
heat for 15 minutes more. Add fresh chives to garnish and a squeeze of
fresh lemon juice.

Turkey & Vegetable Chili

Shared by Laurie Malec, Madison

On a cold, snowy Sunday afternoon, sitting in front of our fireplace, my mother, Barbara Gibbons and I decided to create our own vegetarian chili. The results of that afternoon have been enjoyed by our family and friends for a number of years. This recipe is a wonderful meal, together with all the fixins. Frito scoops, sour cream, shredded cheese and a salad. The perfect dish to take to a friend in need of a pick-me-up! This is a family favorite on a chilly winter day, enjoy!

1	pound ground turkey	1	bunch green onions, sliced
2	tablespoons garlic, crushed	1	large onion, chopped
1	tablespoon cumin	1	10-ounce package mushrooms, sliced
1	tablespoon oregano		
1	teaspoon chili powder	1	28-ounce can crushed tomatoes (with roasted garlic)
1	teaspoon garlic salt		
1 1/2	teaspoons Italian seasoning	3	14 1/2-ounce cans Delmonte zesty tomatoes with jalapeno
1	zucchini, chopped		
1	yellow squash, chopped	1	15-ounce can red kidney beans, drained

Instructions:

In a large dutch oven, brown ground turkey with 1 tablespoon of the garlic until cooked through, breaking turkey into small pieces as it cooks. Drain off excess liquid after turkey is cooked. Sprinkle seasonings over cooked turkey and stir. Add vegetables and 2 tablespoons of garlic to the turkey, cook over medium heat until vegetables are tender. Add tomatoes and beans. Simmer on low heat for 1 hour or place in crock pot on low heat.

Serve with Frito scoops, sour cream and shredded cheddar cheese.

Winter Chili

Shared by Diane Gardner, Madison

3 garlic cloves, chopped
1 large onion, chopped
4-5 tablespoons olive oil
2 teaspoons chili powder
1 teaspoon cumin
1/2 cup ketchup
1 pound hot Italian sausage, chopped
1 pound ground beef
1 small jar sun dried tomatoes, chopped
2 large cans whole tomatoes

1 small red chili pepper, chopped, remove seeds
1 tomato can of water
1 can black beans, drained
1 can red kidney beans, drained
1 can white cannelloni beans, drained
1 can whole kernel corn, drained
salt, to taste
pepper, to taste
cheddar cheese, grated
sour cream

Instructions:

In a large skillet, cook onions and garlic in olive oil, add seasonings, sausage and beef. Cook until sausage and beef are cooked through, and drain off oil. Add sun dried tomatoes, ketchup, cans of tomatoes and water, bring to a boil, let simmer for 20–30 minutes. Remove from heat and add all the beans and corn, return to stove top and simmer for a couple of hours on very low heat. Season with salt and pepper, to taste. If you like it hot, add some red pepper flakes.

Best to make the day before you want to serve it and let it sit overnight. Serve with cheddar cheese and sour cream.

Creamy Ham and Potato Soup

Shared by Susan Ciotti Wivell, Madison

*This is a great alternative to pea soup when you find yourself
with a leftover ham bone!*

1	ham bone	1	cup celery, chopped
2-3	cups potatoes, peeled and cubed	2	cups whole milk
$1/2$	cup onion, chopped and sautéed		salt, to taste
			pepper, to taste
$1/2$	cup bacon, cooked and chopped		chives, to taste
			tarragon, to taste
1	cup carrots, chopped		instant potato flakes, used to thicken soup if needed
1	cup broccoli florets		

Instructions:

In a dutch oven, cover ham bone with water. Boil to make broth. Drain
and remove meat from bone and add broth and meat back to the pot
with uncooked–raw potatoes, onions, carrots, broccoli, celery and
cooked bacon. Add milk and simmer for a couple of hours, adding spices.
Soup will be creamy, add potato flakes to achieve desired thickness.
Garnish with sour cream and cheddar cheese!

Artichoke Blue-Cheese Bisque

Shared by Vilma Roetting Cook, Madison

Soups are easy to prepare for dinner when snuggled down in an anchorage anticipating the beautiful sunset in New England!

1	tablespoon butter	3	cups chicken broth, low salt
1	onion, chopped	$1/4$	teaspoon thyme, dried
$1/3$	cup vermouth	$1/4$	cup whipping cream
2	8-ounce packages frozen artichoke hearts	$1/4$	cup blue cheese, crumbled fresh chives, chopped

Instructions:

Melt butter over medium heat in large saucepan. Add onion and sauté 10 minutes. Add vermouth and simmer until almost all liquid evaporates, about 4 minutes. Add artichoke hearts, chicken broth and thyme. Simmer until artichoke hearts begin to fall apart, about 10 minutes.

Remove from heat and cool slightly. Work in batches and puree soup in blender or food processor until smooth. Pour soup into saucepan, stir in cream and cheese. Simmer over medium heat until cheese melts and soup is smooth, whisking constantly, about 2 minutes.

Ladle into bowls and sprinkle with chives.

Pumpkin Bisque

*Shared by Kelley McMahon, Hopedale, MA
and Kim Castaldo, Madison*

*This is a family tradition
at our Thanksgiving Table!*

⭐

Herb wrap:

1   bay leaf

2   sprigs fresh thyme

2   fresh sage leaves

Bisque:

2   tablespoons unsalted butter

2   leeks, including light green parts, chopped and be sure to rinse thoroughly

2   garlic cloves, chopped

1   celery stalk, diced

1   small onion, diced

3$^1/_2$ cups pumpkin, peeled and diced

1$^1/_2$ quarts chicken broth

1   tablespoon kosher salt

     freshly ground black pepper, to taste

$^1/_4$ cup apple juice

$^1/_4$ cup heavy cream

     croutons, to garnish

     sour cream, to garnish

Instructions:

Make herb wrap by placing all herbs in cheesecloth, wrap with a string, so that herbs can be easily removed from soup. In a medium soup pot, melt the butter over medium heat. Add the leeks, garlic, celery and onion. Cover and cook until the onion is translucent, about 7–10 minutes. Add the pumpkin, herb wrap and chicken broth, bring to a boil. Season with salt and pepper and reduce heat. Cook for 20 minutes or until pumpkin is tender.

Remove the herb wrap. Puree the soup, and return the soup to the pot, add the apple juice and cream. Bring to a simmer and serve warm. Garnish with a dollop of sour cream or croutons.

Cincinnati Chili

Shared by Chris Abbott, Madison

*I got this recipe from a friend in Lenox, MA and it soon became
the chili recipe I made the most, because it takes about 10 minutes
to make and can be eaten right away- no having to let the flavors
blend. My friend gave it the name Cincinnati Chili, so that
is what we have always called it!*

1 pound ground beef	¹/₄ teaspoon nutmeg
1 pound sausage	2 tablespoons chili powder
2 cans tomatoes (1 large and 1 small)	1 teaspoon lemon juice
1 cup tomato sauce or juice	1 teaspoon paprika
1 cup water	¹/₂ teaspoon cinnamon
1 tablespoon brown sugar	¹/₂ teaspoon pepper
2 teaspoons salt	¹/₄ teaspoon mustard
¹/₂ teaspoon celery seed	¹/₄ teaspoon red pepper
	1 bay leaf, crumbled

Instructions:

Brown meat in a large pot, add the rest of the ingredients and simmer for
1 hour or more over medium heat. Watch the liquids and add water if needed.

Asparagus And Crab Meat Soup

Shared by Cassy Pickard, Guilford

This recipe is adapted from a version by Bach Ngo. This is a quick and easy Vietnamese soup that makes a great starter. It is also grand with a tossed salad and crispy bread for lunch or a light supper.

1-2	tablespoons olive oil	2	teaspoons cornstarch dissolved in 3 tablespoons water
1-2	cloves of garlic, finely chopped	1	pound of thin fresh asparagus, chopped $1/2$ inch pieces
2	shallots, finely chopped		
$1/2$	pound fresh crab meat, well picked	1-2	tablespoons fish sauce
$1/2$	teaspoon freshly ground pepper	1	egg, beaten
			fresh cilantro, chopped
1	32-ounce can chicken broth, low sodium		scallion greens, chopped
			salt, to taste
			pepper, to taste

Instructions:

Lightly sauté the garlic and shallots in the oil, do not brown or burn them. Add the crab meat and gently sauté for about 3–4 minutes, do not brown. Sprinkle with $1/2$ teaspoon of pepper over the mixture, add the chicken broth.

When ready to serve, bring soup to a soft boil and add the cornstarch dissolved in the water. Stir well. Add the asparagus and cook until the asparagus is just done, al dente. Add the fish sauce. Adjust seasoning with salt and pepper and more fish sauce as needed to taste.

Immediately before serving, beat the egg and add it to the boiling soup in a long stream held above the pot while stirring the soup. This will allow the egg to cook in long thin strands rather than in clumps like scrambled eggs. Serve in warmed soup bowls. Sprinkle each dish with cilantro and scallions.

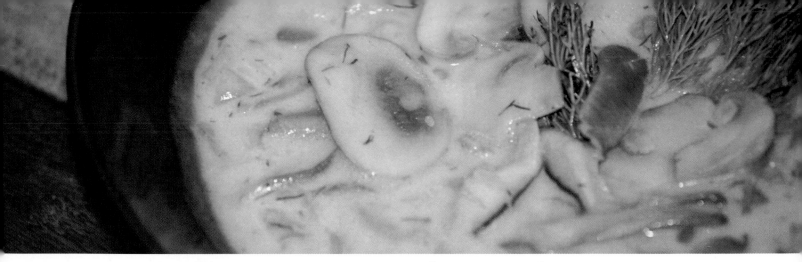

Hungarian Mushroom Soup

Shared by Annie Auerbach, Madison and Amy Miller, Mansfield, MA

Our Dad always made this soup for our tailgating parties before the Buffalo Bills games or after skiing. It is hearty and delicious and easy to make. It serves four, so I usually double the recipe. The first time I made it, I forgot to add the sour cream and actually liked it better.

2 cups onions, chopped

4 tablespoons butter

12 ounce mushrooms, any variety, sliced

2 teaspoons dill weed

2 cups chicken stock

1 tablespoon soy sauce

1 tablespoon paprika

3 tablespoons flour

1 cup milk

1 teaspoon salt

$^1/_2$ cup sour cream

2 teaspoons lemon juice

Instructions:

In a heavy saucepan over medium heat, sauté onions in 2 tablespoons butter. Add mushrooms and dill weed. Add 1 cup chicken stock, soy sauce, paprika and simmer for 15 minutes.

In separate saucepan, melt 2 tablespoons butter and whisk in flour and milk. Cook for 10 minutes or until thick. Stir together with first mixture, add remaining chicken stock.

Simmer 10-15 minutes. Add salt, sour cream and lemon juice. Serve hot!

Chicken and Pappardelle Soup

Shared by Diane Gardner, Madison

This is one of my family's favorite soups. The ultimate comfort soup in the cold of the winter. As soon as the weather turns cool, I start making this.

1	whole chicken	$^1/_4$	cup parmesan cheese
6-7	large carrots, chopped		salt, to taste
1	large package spinach, cleaned, stems removed		pepper, to taste
		1	pound pappardelle pasta

Instructions:

Boil chicken in large soup pot that is filled close to the top with water, this will make the chicken broth. Season chicken broth with salt and pepper. Boil until chicken is tender, remove chicken and de-bone. Put meat back into the broth, if needed add some water. Add carrots and cook until tender, about 10 minutes. Add fresh spinach and bring to a boil.

At this point, turn off stove and add one pound of pasta to hot soup. Add the parmesan cheese and cover. Let stand, the heat will cook the pasta. 15 minutes later soup is ready to serve!

Mississippi 5 Hour Stew

Shared by Dot Reiser, Mystic

This is a hearty stew that my family loves in the winter time! Handed down from my mother of 8, Christine Hackl. It is such a comfort food and it makes a wonderful beef vegetable soup with the leftovers. (See page 82). My mother is from Mississippi, thus giving this tasty stew its name!

2	pounds beef chuck stew meat, cubed	5	carrots, chopped, 1/2 inch or smaller
1	can Campbell's condensed tomato soup	1	large white onion, chopped 1/2 inch or smaller
1	can Campbell's beef broth	3	potatoes, peeled and cubed
5	stalks celery, chopped, 1/2 inch or smaller		salt, to taste
			pepper, to taste

Instructions:

Put everything into a casserole, cover and cook on 250 degrees for 5 hours. Tastes better the second day after the flavors have blended.

Liz's
Sweet and Spicy Chili

Shared by Liz Wallack, Madison

Bringing home 3rd place, this award winning chili is one to make! At the First Annual Chili Cook-off for The Friends of Madison Youth, this was one of the top favorites by over 300 people! It is simple to make and a delicious meal on a cold winter night.

3	pounds ground hamburger
	olive oil
1	small onion, chopped finely
1	green pepper, chopped finely
1	16-ounce jar salsa, medium hot
1	28-ounce can B&M baked beans w/bacon, onion & brown sugar
6	ounce can tomato paste
1	14$\frac{1}{2}$ ounce can tomato w/zesty jalapenos, diced
1	tablespoon chili powder
4	ounces taco sauce
1	tablespoon taco seasoning mix
	hot sauce, to taste

Instructions:

Sauté onion and green pepper in olive oil until soft. Add hamburger meat and cook until brown. Drain all excess liquid. Add all remaining ingredients and transfer to a crock pot and cook for about 1–2 hours.

Serve with cheese and sour cream.

Barbara Barker's Chili

Shared by Barbara Barker, Madison

2	tablespoons peanut oil
2	pounds hot Italian sausage, remove casings
1¹/₂	pounds hamburger meat
2	pounds boneless pork loin chops, cut into ¹/₂ inch pieces
1	16-ounce jar hot salsa
2	large onions, chopped
3	heaping teaspoons garlic, chopped
1	bag frozen green bell peppers, chopped
1	14-ounce can sweet red roasted peppers, drained and chopped
4	14-ounce cans diced tomatoes with smoked chilis
1	28-ounce can tomato puree
4	14-ounce cans pinto beans, rinsed and drained
1	4-ounce can diced chilies
1	teaspoon coriander
1	teaspoon cumin
1¹/₂	teaspoon oregano
¹/₃	cup chili powder
	cayenne, to taste (start with ¹/₂ teaspoon)
	red pepper flakes, to taste
4	tablespoons brown sugar

Instructions:

Heat peanut oil and add sausage, hamburger and pork, cook until done. Drain fat and stir in salsa. In separate fry pan, sauté onions, garlic, green peppers and red roasted peppers. Transfer meat and onion mixture to a large 3 gallon cast iron pot. Add the remaining ingredients and stir.

After everything is cooking slowly in pot add 4 tablespoons brown sugar. Cook for 3 to 4 hours on low temperature, stirring with a wooden spoon. Chili is better after a day in the refrigerator, allowing flavors to blend.

Voted the Number 1 chili at the First Annual Chili Cook-off. Barbara loves to cook and after tasting this chili, you will agree that she knows how to make a great chili. This chili is a crowd pleaser and will feed a large group!

Chili Con Carne

Shared by Lisa McAndrews, Madison

1	tablespoon vegetable oil
2	pounds ground beef
1	cup onion, chopped coarsely
1/4	cup green or red pepper, chopped (any kind of chili pepper can be used)
2	large garlic cloves, minced
1	16-ounce can chopped tomatoes
1	16-ounce can tomato sauce
1	package "Old El Paso" chili seasoning mix (secret ingredient!)
1	teaspoon cumin dash of cayenne pepper
1	16-ounce can dark red kidney beans
1	16-ounce can black beans monterey jack or cheddar cheese salt, to taste

Award winning chili that earned 2nd place in the 1st Annual Chili Cook-off for The Friends of Madison Youth. This chili is so easy to make, no fancy ingredients are used and I get rave reviews every time I make it, especially from my husband Jim!

Instructions:

Begin 2 hours before you plan to serve.

In a large Dutch oven, heat oil and add ground meat, onions, peppers and garlic. Cook over medium heat until onion is translucent. Drain most of the liquid and return Dutch oven back to burner. Add canned tomatoes, tomato sauce, chili seasoning mix, cumin and cayenne pepper. Remove from heat and drain liquid, stir in beans. Simmer 15–30 minutes more and serve with cheese. This will serve 6–8.

Hearty Beef Barley Soup

Shared by Michael Cardillo, Jr. Innkeeper, The Old Mystic Inn, Mystic

When we were growing up, my mom used to make this soup all the time. When she went to add the barley, she always thought she hadn't added quite enough so she continued to add more barley. By the time the soup was cooked, the wooden spoon could stand up alone in the middle of the pot! Remember that barley, rice and pastas will absorb the liquid in the recipe if you add too much. Mom finally perfected her creation and here it is!

2	tablespoons olive oil	1	cup green beans, diced
1/2	cup onion, chopped	1	32-ounce can beef broth (homemade or all natural)
2	tablespoons garlic, minced	1	cup water
1/2	cup green pepper, chopped	1	sprig fresh rosemary
1 1/2	pounds cubed beef, cut in 1 inch thick pieces (blade steak works best)	1/2	teaspoon marjoram
2	cups carrots, diced	1/2	cup barley
2	cups celery, diced		salt, to taste
2	cups mushrooms, chopped		pepper, to taste

Instructions:

In a medium sized pot, over medium heat, heat the olive oil and sauté the onion, garlic and peppers. Add the beef and sauté until slightly browned, about 5 minutes. Add the rest of the ingredients except the barley and let the soup cook until all vegetables and beef are tender, at least one hour, over medium-low heat. Finally, add the barley, salt and pepper, and cook until the barley is done.

Hearty Beef Vegetable Soup

Shared by Dot Reiser, Mystic

**This is a great quick and easy meal to make with leftovers
of my Mississippi 5 Hour Stew, page 77.**

left-over Mississippi 5 Hour Stew, chopped into small bites	1 bag mixed frozen vegetables (corn, lima, carrot mix)
1 large can stewed tomatoes	1 small cabbage, sliced fine
1 can beef broth	salt, to taste
	pepper, to taste

Instructions:

Combine all the ingredients in large soup pot and bring to a boil. Reduce
heat and simmer on low for 1 hour.

**Serve with a loaf of crusty bread and salad for a wonderful meal on a chilly
New England night.*

New England Clam Chowder

Shared by Don Knight, Stamford

This has been a family tradition on Christmas Eve as long as I can remember. I always bring a large pot of this delicious clam chowder to our family gathering. This is the perfect comfort food on a cold Christmas Eve.

4	dozen little neck clams or cherry stone clams	1	medium onion, chopped fine
1	cup water	1	28-ounce can potatoes, chopped medium
2	stalks celery	$1^1/_2$	cups whole milk
1	clove garlic	2	stalks celery, chopped fine
$^1/_4$	pound bacon, cooked crispy, chopped		roux-4 tablespoons flour, add water to make thick paste

Instructions:

Place clams in saucepan with a cup of water, 2 stalks celery and garlic. Cook until clams open, discard celery and garlic. Let clams cool and chop, set aside. Reserve clam liquid.

Cook bacon until crispy and set aside. In bacon fat, sauté onion and cook until soft, add potatoes. Add juice from cooking clams and heat thoroughly. Then add milk and bring almost to a boil. Add celery, salt and freshly ground pepper.

When broth is almost to a boil, add roux in a little at a time, stirring constantly. The soup will thicken slowly. When it reaches the boiling point, add cooked, chopped clams. You're done!

winter vegetables, salads & side dishes

Winter Meets Spring Salad

Palmer's Traditional Steak Fries

Cauliflower and Goat Cheese Gratin

Scalloped Potatoes

Sweet Potato Casserole

Pineapple Soufflé

Carol's Macaroni and Cheese

Oven Roasted Potatoes

Mexican Salad

Egg Noodle Pudding

Spicy Spinach

Sweet Corn and Thyme Pudding

Corn Casserole

Mrs. Euroff's Pot Luck Beans

Lentils & Rice

Praline Yam Casserole

Cranberry Grand Marnier Relish

Cranberry Chutney

Spiced Cranberries

Stuffed Phyllo Cups

Roasted Asparagus

Parmesan and Onion Risotto

Stuffed Baked Potatoes

Nanny's Stuffed Artichokes

Holiday Brussel Sprouts with Roasted Nuts

Green Beans Almondine

Potato Latkes

Wild Mushroom Tart

winter vegetables, salads & side dishes

Winter Meets Spring Salad

Shared by Chef Robert Crimm, S-Car-Go, Old Lyme

1 pound walnuts	¹/₄ cup blueberries, fresh
¹/₄ cup balsamic vinaigrette	¹/₄ cup apricots, dried
¹/₂ cup white sugar	¹/₄ cup gorgonzola cheese
1 bag mixed salad greens	¹/₄ cup cranberries, dried
1 green apple, sliced and tossed with lemon juice	balsamic vinaigrette dressing

Instructions:

To caramelize the walnuts, place in a small bowl, combine walnuts, balsamic vinaigrette and sugar. Toss to coat, and then spread walnuts out on a flat cookie sheet. Roast in a 350 degree oven for about 10 minutes. Be sure to stir every few minutes so that they don't burn. Cooking time may take longer than 10 minutes, you want to be sure that the sugar is completely melted and the walnuts are covered with a golden brown glaze. Let cool and break apart with your hands. You may want to make extra as the family will eat them until they are gone!

On a large platter, make a bed out of greens. Top with apple slices, blueberries, apricots, cheese, cranberries and then walnuts. Drizzle balsamic vinaigrette over the top.

Palmer's Traditional Steak Fries

Shared by Zandra Baker, Palmer's Market, Darien

3	Idaho potatoes	olive oil, to coat fries
1	clove garlic, minced	salt, to taste
1	tablespoon parsley, chopped	pepper, to taste

Instructions:

Preheat oven to 350 degrees. Wash potatoes and cut into spears, 8 or 6 per potato depending on size of potato. In a medium sized bowl, combine garlic, parsley, olive oil, salt and pepper. Place potatoes in bowl and toss to completely coat. Line potatoes on a sheet pan and bake for 15-20 minutes.

Cauliflower and Goat Cheese Gratin

Shared by Amy Vrzal, Stamford

1 head cauliflower,
cut into florets

2 cups heavy cream

1/2 pound monterey jack cheese,
coarsely grated

2 cups parmesan cheese, grated

6 ounces goat cheese,
cut into small pieces

salt, to taste

pepper, to taste

Instructions:

Preheat oven to 400 degrees. In a medium casserole dish, layer the cauliflower, heavy cream and three cheeses. Season with salt and pepper. Roast for 20–30 minutes or until the cauliflower is soft and the sauce has thickened slightly. Remove from the oven and let rest for 10 minutes before serving.

Scalloped Potatoes

Shared by Kym Scott, Guilford

This in one of my families' favorite comfort foods. We serve it during the holidays with baked ham and roasted meats.

6-8	large baking potatoes	2	cups milk
1/2	stick of butter	8	ounces cheddar cheese, sharp
1/4	cup flour	1/4	cup breadcrumbs

Instructions:

Bake potatoes, cool and peel. Slice potatoes and layer into a large baking pan. In a small saucepan melt butter over medium low heat and slowly mix in flour, milk and cheese. Stir until nice and thick and starting to bubble. Pour cheese mixture over potatoes and sprinkle with breadcrumbs. Bake for one hour in a 350 degree oven.

Sweet Potato Casserole

Shared by Liz Crowther, Madison

2$^1/_4$ pounds sweet potatoes, peeled, washed and quartered

$^1/_3$ cup brown sugar, packed

$^1/_3$ cup fat free milk

2 tablespoons reduced calorie margarine, melted (I prefer Willow Run soy margarine)

1 teaspoon vanilla extract

$^1/_2$ teaspoon salt

2 large eggs, beaten lightly

Topping:

$^1/_2$ cup brown sugar, packed

$^1/_4$ cup all purpose flour

2 tablespoons chilled margarine

$^1/_3$ cup pecans, chopped

Instructions:

Cook sweet potatoes in a large pot of boiling water until tender, about 20 minutes, then remove from heat and mash. Remove potatoes from water and combine in a large bowl with brown sugar, milk, margarine, vanilla, salt and eggs. Coat an 8 inch square baking dish with cooking spray and fold potato mixture into it. In a small bowl, combine first 2 topping ingredients. Cut margarine into mixture with 2 knives, until mixture resembles coarse meal. Stir in pecans and sprinkle this mixture over the sweet potato mixture. Bake for 30 minutes in a 350 degree oven. This dish serves 8.

Pineapple Soufflé

Shared by Gretchen Matkin, Madison

1$^1/_2$ cups butter, softened

1 cup sugar

4 eggs

1 large can crushed pineapple, drained

5 slices Pepperidge Farm toasting bread (Dutentine), cubed

Instructions:

Cream butter and sugar. Beat in eggs one at a time. Fold in pineapple. Fold in bread cubes. Turn into 1$^1/_2$ quart buttered casserole. Bake uncovered for 1 hour at 350 degrees. Watch carefully! This is great with ham.

Carol's Macaroni and Cheese

Shared by Amy Woodford, Old Saybrook

$^2/_3$ pound Cabot cheddar cheese, extra sharp
1 pound Prince ziti
6 tablespoons butter
6 tablespoons flour
1 quart 2 percent milk
2 jars Old English cheese
   salt, to taste
   pepper, to taste

Topping:

3 tablespoons butter
$^2/_3$ cup breadcrumbs
   salt, to taste
   pepper, to taste

Instructions:

Shred cheddar cheese and set aside. Cook ziti according to package instructions. In a medium saucepan, heat butter until melted, remove from heat and stir in flour to form a paste. Gradually stir in milk. Place saucepan on medium high heat and stir in Old English cheese. Sauce should thicken, season with salt and pepper.

In an oblong casserole dish, spread one layer of ziti, cover with shredded cheese and repeat with a second layer. After final layer, top with cooked cheese mixture, this should cover the ziti, if not, press ziti down so that the sauce covers the pasta.

To make the topping, melt butter in fry pan, add breadcrumbs, salt and pepper to coat. Sprinkle topping on top of ziti.

Bake at 365 degrees for approximately 45 minutes, until brown and bubbly. Let sit for a few minutes before serving.

Oven Roasted Potatoes

Shared by Sharon D'Amico, Madison

*Potatoes in any shape or form are my comfort food.
My husband attributes this to my Irish ancestry. This recipe,
however, I learned from my Italian father-in-law. Enjoy!*

4-6 large potatoes, washed and peeled	salt, to taste
$^3/_4$ cup vegetable oil	pepper, to taste
2-3 garlic cloves, sliced	3 tablespoons butter
	Italian seasoning, to taste

Instructions:

Cut potatoes into bite sized pieces and place in a 13 x 9 inch baking dish. Toss potatoes with oil and add garlic, salt and pepper. Toss again and dot with butter. Sprinkle top of potatoes with Italian seasoning. Bake for 1 hour at 350 degrees, turning every 20 minutes or so. Put potatoes under the broiler for the final 4–6 minutes to brown them up.

Mexican Salad

Shared by Don Fowler, Stamford

A recipe of the late Kaye Fowler, and a family favorite!

1 head of lettuce	1 large avocado
1 bunch green onions or 1 bunch medium purple onions or green hot peppers, for those daring souls (substitute salsa)	1 regular can Pet milk (can substitute Carnation)
	1 pound Velveeta cheese
1 large ripe tomato	1 large bag Doritos
	lemon juice

Instructions:

The night before serving, mix avocado, onion and juice of one lemon. Chop and stir until it becomes a fine spread. Let set covered overnight.

Shred head of lettuce in large mixing bowl. Add chopped tomatoes and avocado mix. Mix gently. In saucepan, blend Velveeta and canned milk, heat until blended.

Mash Doritos in bag. Pour Doritos over salad. Pour cheese sauce over salad mix. Stir all together. Serve hot.

Egg Noodle Pudding

Shared by Valerie Engstrom, Branford

This recipe was given to me by a fellow nurse when I worked at the Greenwich hospital many years ago. In the Jewish religion it is referred to as a kugel and usually contains raisins and other variations.

1	8-ounce package wide egg noodles, cooked according to package instructions	1/2	cup sugar
1	cup sour cream	1	tablespoon lemon juice
1/4	pound cottage cheese, about 4-ounces		**Topping**
1/4	pound butter, melted	1/2	stick butter, melted
2	eggs, beaten	1/4	cup sugar
		1	teaspoon cinnamon
		1 1/2	cups corn flakes, crushed

Instructions:

Spray a 10 inch square pan with cooking spray. Combine first 7 ingredients and fold into pan. For topping, combine all ingredients and spread on top of noodle mixture. Bake at 350 degrees for one hour. *This recipe serves 6.*

Spicy Spinach

Shared by The Cooking Co, Killingworth

1	package baby spinach	2	cloves garlic, chopped
2	tablespoons toasted sesame oil	2	tablespoons sesame seeds
1/4	teaspoon red pepper flakes, crushed		salt, to taste

Instructions:

Combine all ingredients in a bowl. Spread on a baking tray and place in a preheated oven (350 degrees) for 3–5 minutes or until spinach begins to wilt. Place spinach on a plate and top with salmon. Found on page 128.

This recipe serves 4-6.

Sweet Corn and Thyme Pudding

Shared by Aux Delices Foods, Stamford

4	cups corn kernels (from 6–7 ears)	2	tablespoons thyme leaves, fresh
6	eggs		
1	cup heavy cream	1¼	teaspoons sea salt
1	cup milk	¼	teaspoon freshly ground pepper
½	cup all purpose flour	1	tablespoon butter, unsalted

Instructions:

Place 2 cups of corn in a blender, add eggs, cream, milk, thyme, flour, salt and pepper. Cover this with a towel. Pulse a few times and then process on low until the mixture is smooth. Lightly butter 8 individual ramekins. Mix together the corn mixture and remaining 2 cups of corn in a medium sized bowl. Spoon this mixture into the ramekins until they are about three-quarters full. Place the ramekins into a roasting pan and put it in the oven. Pour hot water into the roasting pan until it reaches halfway up the ramekins. Bake the pudding for one hour in a 350 degree oven. Rotate the pan once 180 degrees halfway through the cooking process. The pudding is done when the center is firm and the top is golden brown.

Corn Casserole

Shared by Barbara Gibbons, Madison

1	medium onion, chopped	$^1/_4$	teaspoon salt
4	tablespoons butter		dash of pepper
2	eggs	$^1/_2$	package Jiffy corn muffin mix, about $^3/_4$ cup
1	can creamed corn	1	cup sour cream
1	can whole corn, drained	1	cup cheddar cheese, shredded

Instructions:

In a small sauce pan, sauté onion in butter and set aside. In a medium bowl, combine eggs, corn, spices, and muffin mix. Spray casserole dish with cooking spray and fold egg mixture into casserole. Spread onions over egg mixture, then spread sour cream and finally cheese over the sour cream. Bake for 30 minutes in a 400 degree oven.

Mrs. Euroff's Pot Luck Beans

Shared by Billy Budd, Madison

This was a big hit at Hunter's little league cookout. This is a recipe from Maggie, the wife of one of the coaches.

2	16-18-ounce cans baking beans	1	teaspoon dry mustard
$^3/_4$ cup brown sugar		6	slices bacon, chopped
		$^1/_2$	cup ketchup

Instructions:

Spread can of beans in pan. Mix brown sugar and mustard together and sprinkle half of this mixture over the beans. Top with bacon, then ketchup. Sprinkle the rest of brown sugar mixture on top. Bake $1^1/_2$ to 2 hours at 350 degrees.

Lentils & Rice

Shared by Anne Rakocy, Madison
Good Italian comfort food!

2	tablespoons olive oil	1	48-ounce can chicken broth
1	onion, chopped	1	cup uncooked rice
4-5	cloves garlic, chopped	1	14$\frac{1}{2}$-ounce can chicken broth
1	celery rib, chopped	1	8-ounce can tomato sauce
2	carrots, chopped		Parmigiano-Reggiano cheese, to taste
1	cup dry lentils		

Instructions:

In a large pot, sauté onion, garlic, celery and carrots in olive oil until onion is wilted. Add lentils & large chicken broth. Bring to boil, cover tightly & simmer 25–30 minutes.

Add rice & additional chicken broth. Cover and cook 15–20 minutes or until rice is cooked. (Longer if using brown rice, but white is better in this dish.)

Add tomato sauce, salt and pepper. Simmer for 5 minutes. Sprinkle generously with grated Parmigiano-Reggiano cheese. Add more chicken broth or water if too dry.

Praline Yam Casserole

Shared by Carol Kenyhercz, Branford

6 medium yams or sweet potatoes
$^1/_2$ cup butter
1 teaspoon baking powder
1 teaspoon cinnamon
1 teaspoon vanilla
2 eggs
$^1/_4$ cup granulated sugar
$^3/_4$ cup buttermilk**

Topping:

1 cup brown sugar
$^1/_4$ cup flour
4 tablespoons butter, softened
1 cup pecans, chopped

This is a favorite of mine…it's always a hit, a fancy way to serve yams/sweet potatoes. This is wonderful when serving roasted pork, chicken and turkey. The kids love it! I have included my little shortcut for making buttermilk, rather than the real thing. I've used this in a pinch, when I did not have buttermilk on hand.

Instructions:

**In a pinch you can make buttermilk by adding 3–4 tablespoons of wine vinegar to $^3/_4$ cup milk, but real buttermilk is preferred.

Cook yams or sweet potatoes until tender, peel and mash. Add butter and remaining ingredients, beating thoroughly with a mixer. The potatoes are much creamier when beat with a mixer. Spray casserole dish with Pam and add potato mixture.

To make topping, combine brown sugar, flour and softened butter until crumbly. Add pecans and sprinkle on top. Bake at 350 degrees for 30 minutes.

Cranberry Grand Marnier Relish

Shared by Christine Chesanek, Old Saybrook

This is a Fromage exclusive, our holiday relish that is delicious with poultry or fish, a nice addition to your festive table.

$^1/_2$	of one orange	$1^1/_4$ cups sugar	
2	cups water	$^1/_2$	teaspoon cinnamon, ground
1	Granny Smith apple	$^1/_4$	teaspoon cloves, ground
3	cups cranberries, fresh	$^1/_4$	cup Grand Marnier liquor

Instructions:

Squeeze the juice of the orange and set aside. Remove the membrane from inside of the orange and discard. Cut the outer "shell" of the orange into very small dices. Put these into a small saucepan with water and bring to a boil for 10 minutes. Drain and set aside. Peel, quarter and core the apple. Chop apple into small pieces and place in a saucepan. Sort through cranberries, discarding any soft ones. Place cranberries in the saucepan with the apple, diced orange peel, reserved orange juice, sugar, cinnamon, cloves and Grand Marnier. Bring this to a boil, reduce heat to simmer and cover partially. Simmer gently, stir occasionally until the sauce has thickened, the apple is tender and the cranberries have begun to burst, about 10–15 minutes.

Transfer to a bowl and let cool before serving. This can also be covered, refrigerated and brought to room temperature before serving.

This recipe makes $3^1/_2$ to 4 cups of relish.

Cranberry Chutney

Shared by Barbara Gibbons, Madison

A delicious cranberry chutney with apples, oranges, golden raisins and spices, perfect alongside pork, turkey or chicken!

1 orange, peeled, tough membranes removed, chopped	$^1/_2$ cup golden raisins
$^1/_4$ cup orange juice	$^1/_4$ cup pecans or walnuts, chopped
1 package fresh cranberries	1 tablespoon apple cider vinegar
$1^3/_4$ cups sugar	$^1/_2$ teaspoon ginger, ground
1 large golden delicious apple, peeled, cored and chopped	$^1/_2$ teaspoon cinnamon, ground

Instructions:

Combine all ingredients in a large saucepan and bring to a boil. Reduce heat and let simmer, stirring occasionally for 5–8 minutes or until cranberries begin to burst. Chill until serving time and freeze surplus for later use in small containers. Makes 4 cups of chutney.

Spiced Cranberries

Shared by Chris Abbot, Madison

This is one of the recipes I cherish from my grandmother. It is very simple to make, it fills the house with wonderful aromas and it is a great addition to our Thanksgiving dinner.

2 quarts cranberries, fresh	2 tablespoons cinnamon, ground
$1^1/_3$ cups white vinegar	
$^2/_3$ cup water	1 tablespoon cloves, ground
6 cups sugar	1 tablespoon allspice

Instructions:

Wash and pick over berries. In a large saucepan, place berries and all remaining ingredients. Bring the mixture to a boil and then simmer for 45 minutes or longer.

This makes 3 pints.

Stuffed Phyllo Cups

Shared by Diane Gardner and Kim Castaldo, Madison

These little Phyllo cups make a wonderful addition to your favorite salad. Serve them warm on top of the salad for an unexpected delightful bite!

3-4 tablespoons butter	salt, to taste
2-3 leeks, washed well, chopped	pepper, to taste
6-8 ounces goat cheese or gorgonzola	1 box phyllo cups, frozen
3-4 tablespoons sour cream	1/4 cup parmesan cheese, grated

Instructions:

Melt butter in sauté pan, add leeks and cook until crunchy and tender. Transfer leeks to a mixing bowl, add goat cheese, sour cream, parmesan cheese and salt and pepper. Fill phyllo cups with leek–cheese mixture, top with parmesan cheese and bake for 10–12 minutes in a 350 degree oven until tops are golden brown.

Roasted Asparagus

Shared by Stuart London, Branford

*This is one of my favorite, simple and delicious recipes.
Using good Italian Parmesan or Grana Padano Parmesan cheese
in this dish makes all the difference.*

1 pound asparagus, washed, tough ends removed	1 teaspoon black pepper, freshly ground
1/4 cup fruity extra virgin olive oil	zest from 1 lemon
1 tablespoon garlic, finely minced	1/2 cup Parmigiano-Reggiano cheese, grated or Grana Padano Parmesan cheese
1 teaspoon sea salt	

Instructions:

Preheat oven to 450 degrees. In a large bowl toss the asparagus with olive oil, garlic, salt, pepper and lemon zest. Arrange asparagus in an oven proof platter and pour any remaining oil mixture over the asparagus. Coat with some of the grated cheese, roast asparagus in oven for 5 minutes. Toss the asparagus again, top with remaining cheese and roast for another 10 minutes. Cheese should be melted and slightly browned. This can be served with lemon wedges or a drizzle of good aged balsamic vinegar.

Parmesan and Onion Risotto

Shared by Lee White, Old Lyme

1	quart chicken stock, low sodium	1	cup good white wine
3	tablespoons olive oil	4	tablespoons butter, unsalted
1	small onion, finely diced	1	cup Parmigiano-Reggiano cheese, grated
1½	cups Arborio rice		truffle oil, optional

Instructions:

Pour chicken stock in a pot and let simmer. In a large heavy skillet, heat olive oil and sauté onions until translucent but not browned. Add rice and sauté for about 45 seconds. Add 2 cups of chicken stock, stir and cover with lid. Bring heat to high and in about 4–5 minutes, remove lid and stir rice with a wooden spoon. If the stock is completely absorbed, add another cup of stock and begin to stir, keeping the heat high. Continue to add stock until rice no longer will absorb anymore. The rice should be somewhat chewy but not hard. Remove from heat, add butter and stir. Add Parmigiano-Reggiano cheese and stir and add truffle oil to taste if desired. Serve immediately.

Stuffed Baked Potatoes

Shared by Diane Dolan, Madison

5	medium baking potatoes	1	teaspoon onion salt
½	cup sour cream	⅛	teaspoon pepper
1	3-ounce package cream cheese, softened	5	pieces bacon, fried and chopped
2	tablespoons milk	¼	cup cheddar cheese, grated
2	tablespoons butter, softened	⅛	teaspoon pepper

Instructions:

Wash and bake potatoes for 70–80 minutes in a 375 degree oven. Cut the top of each potato off and scoop out inside of potato. In a small bowl, mash together potato, sour cream, cream cheese, milk, butter, salt and pepper. Beat until smooth and fluffy. Fill potato shells with potato mixture and return to oven. Bake uncovered for 15 minutes, add bacon and cheddar cheese to top, if desired.

Nanny's Stuffed Artichokes

Shared by Chris Rinere, Madison

I will warn you, these are truly a labor of love. My Nanny would make these on special occasions and always for me because she knew how much I loved them. After spending much time in Nanny's kitchen, I continued to pick up on little tricks that she applied to her cooking. The drizzling of the olive oil is one of her tricks…don't skimp!

6	large artichokes	2	tablespoons parsley, dried
3	cups Italian breadcrumbs	6	cloves garlic, chopped fine
1	cup parmesan cheese	6	tablespoons olive oil

Instructions:

Cut off the stalk of each artichoke so that they can sit on the counter by themselves. Trim about one inch off the top, so that the top is flat. Bang them on the counter flat side down to open the leaves, rinse with water, pat dry and set aside. In a medium bowl, mix breadcrumbs, cheese, parsley and garlic. With a spoon, stuff as many of the leaves as possible with the breadcrumb filling. Sit the stuffed artichokes in a Dutch oven that has approximately 2 inches of water in it. Drizzle 1 tablespoon olive oil over each artichoke. Cover and simmer on the stove for one hour, always making sure that at least 1¹/₂ inches of water remain in the Dutch oven. Artichokes are done when the leaves are tender and can be pulled without effort. Transfer artichokes to a baking dish and cook, covered for 15 minutes in a 350 degree oven. Remove foil and cook for a final 5 minutes. These are great served warm or at room temperature.

Holiday Brussel Sprouts with Roasted Nuts

Shared by Diane Gardner and Kim Castaldo, Madison

We were cooking in the kitchen one day, and this is one of the recipes that we came up with.

1$^{1}/_{2}$ pounds fresh brussel sprouts
$^{1}/_{2}$ cup olive oil
2 tablespoons white wine
1 tablespoon Dijon mustard
3 tablespoons red wine vinegar
2 teaspoons sugar

salt, to taste
pepper, to taste
15 cherry tomatoes, washed
1 cup walnuts or pecans roasted in oven, chopped

Instructions:

Steam brussel sprouts in boiling water until tender, about 8 minutes. Transfer to serving bowl, keep warm. Combine olive oil, white wine, mustard, vinegar, sugar, salt and pepper, mix thoroughly. Transfer olive oil mixture to saucepan and cook over medium heat until completely heated. Toss cherry tomatoes in for one last minute. Pour entire mixture over brussel sprouts and top with roasted nuts. Serve warm. *This recipe serves 6.*

Green Beans Almondine

Shared by Andrew T. Speziale,
The Sand Castle at The Surf Club, Madison

**This classic French dish is the perfect accompaniment
to any holiday meal.**

1	pound green beans, washed, stems removed	3	ounces almonds, sliced
3	ounces butter	2	ounces fresh parsley
1	ounce shallots, chopped		salt, to taste
			pepper, to taste

Instructions:

Blanch green beans in lightly salted water for 4 minutes. Cool in ice bath and set aside. Melt butter in a deep sided, heavy skillet over medium heat. Once butter is melted, angle pan to one side so that the butter pools. Keep heat on medium and set pan flat on burner, butter will brown instantly. Immediately add shallots and almonds to pan, sautée over medium heat until shallots are translucent. Add parsley, salt and pepper and stir. Add green beans and toss to coat in butter mixture until heated through. Adjust salt and pepper to taste.

If shallots are unavailable you may substitute red onion, use $1/2$ an ounce.

Potato Latkes

Shared by Stuart London, Branford

1   pound red skin potatoes, peeled
     and shredded

1/2 pound mashed potatoes

1/2 pound onions, finely minced
     (can substitute scallions)

4   eggs, beaten

1   cup matzo meal

1   tablespoon salt

1   tablespoon pepper

1/2 teaspoon fresh nutmeg, grated

1/4 teaspoon cayenne pepper
     potato or corn starch as needed
     peanut or vegetable oil,
     for frying

This is my mom's family recipe for the traditional potato pancakes served at Passover and other holidays. The thing I really love about this recipe is that the cakes are thick and crispy on the outside and creamy and potatoey on the inside. I like to make a large batch and freeze them so I can have them anytime with sour cream and applesauce.

Instructions:

In a strainer, squeeze out the liquid from the shredded potatoes. In a large bowl, mix all ingredients thoroughly. The mix should have the consistency of thick mashed potatoes. If you need to stiffen the mix, add a little of the starch at a time until it's just right. You do not want the pancakes to spread out when frying, you want them to remain thick. Pan fry in 1 inch of oil on medium heat, flip to crisp both sides. Pancakes need to fry in oil long enough to cook, but be careful not to burn them. I make them about 2–3 ounces each in size. Serve with sour cream.

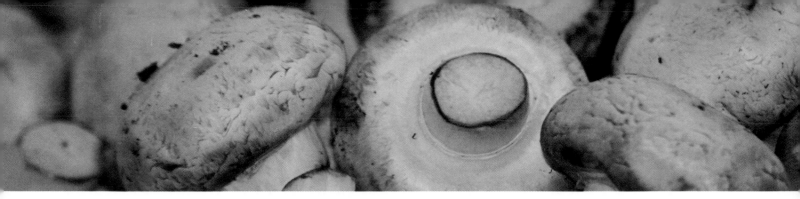

Wild Mushroom Tart

Shared by The Silvermine Tavern, Norwalk

Often referred to as the most romantic inn on the shoreline, the Silvermine Tavern is sought after for its wonderful food and country store.

1 cup dry morrell mushrooms	1 cup shitake mushrooms, fresh
2 cups cold water	1 cup porcini mushrooms, fresh
2 cups beef stock	1 cup black trumpet mushrooms, fresh
1 quart heavy cream	
salt, to taste	1 cup hen of the woods mushrooms, fresh
pepper, to taste	
2 tablespoons butter, unsalted	10 slices Westfield Farms aged blue goat cheese (or any other cheese of your choice)
1 tablespoon shallots, diced	

Instructions:

Soak Morrell mushrooms in 2 cups cold water for 24 hours. Drain mushroom liquid into a 2 quart sauce pot, heat on medium heat until it is reduced to a glaze. Add beef stock and continue cooking until reduced by half. This should amount to approximately 1 cup of Morrell reduction. Remove 1/2 cup of reduction and set aside. Add cream to remaining 1/2 cup of reduction and reduce by half over medium heat. Season this Morrell sauce with salt and pepper to taste. In a large sauté pan, heat butter over medium heat and add diced shallots, cooking until soft, about 2 minutes. Add the 4 different types of mushrooms and continue to cook for 5 minutes, stir frequently so as not to burn. Add 1/2 cup of Morrell reduction and reduce until there is a glaze on the mushrooms, season with salt and pepper. Fill 10 tart shells with the hot mushroom ragout. Drizzle a small amount of the Morrell cream sauce over the mushrooms. Place a slice of cheese on top of the mushrooms and cook in a 350 degree oven until cheese melts, about 3–4 minutes.

simply seafood & pasta dishes

Red Wine Pasta

Spaghetti Al Crudo with Crispy Tilapia

Fresh Herbed Angel Hair Pasta

Vodka Sauce

Chef Lou's Fettuccine

Bolognese Sauce

Spaghetti with Fresh Sardines

Baked Salmon with Saffron

Shrimp, It's Hot, Hot, Hot!

Cliff's Chicken Rigatoni

Garlic Shrimp w/Plum Tomatoes & Pesto over Pappardelle

Baked Stuffed Manicotti

Cioppino

Sesame Crusted Salmon with Spicy Spinach

Super Salmon Cakes

Mussels in White Clam Sauce

Baked Tilapia with Sourdough Bread crumbs

Baked Flounder with Shallots

Seafood Casserole

Baked Black Cod

Sea Scallops w/Apple Smoked Bacon & Wild Mushroom Ragout

Sicilian Supper

Thompson's Baked Swordfish

Scallops on Spinach with Apple Brandy Sauce

Lazy Lobster

Fish with Grapes

Tilapia Medeterrani

simply seafood & pasta dishes

Red Wine Pasta

Shared by Cassy Pickard, Guilford

This recipe is adapted from Mark Bittman. This is an unusual preparation for pasta. It is similar to making risotto. One of the fun benefits of this simple preparation is that no one will be expecting its lovely rose color. Be sure to serve it with foods that set off the color. Fish, chicken and definitely a green salad are good choices. Meats tend to appear drab next to the colorful spaghetti.

1	pound of spaghetti, dried not fresh	1	750 ml bottle of a decent red wine
2	cloves garlic, chopped	1	tablespoon butter
1	shallot or $^{1}/_{2}$ onion, chopped		cilantro and/or basil for presentation
2	tablespoons olive oil		parmesan cheese, grated

Instructions:

Bring well salted water to a boil in a pot large enough for the pasta. Meanwhile, sauté the garlic and shallots in olive oil in a skillet large enough to hold the pasta. Add $^{1}/_{4}$ of the bottle of wine to the garlic mixture. Let that simmer on a low temperature. Add the pasta to the boiling water. The trick here is NOT to cook the pasta. Rather, once the pasta has begun to soften, lift it from the water with tongs. Do not drain the pasta, you want the extra starch clinging to the pasta to be included. The pasta should be just cooked enough that it is hanging limply from the tongs, no more than that.

Add the pasta to the garlic-wine mixture. Stir well to mix all the wine through the pasta. Add another $^{1}/_{4}$ of the bottle of wine. Stir to mix and continue to cook on medium. As the wine is reduced, keep adding additional wine from the bottle to the pasta. The pasta will continue to cook in the liquid and take on a lovely rose color. Continue this process until the full bottle of wine has been used. If the pasta seems too liquid, just reduce it. When it is al dente, stir in the butter. This will give the pasta a wonderful sheen. Adjust the taste with salt and pepper. Lift with tongs to a warmed serving bowl or to individual plates. Pour any additional sauce over pasta. Top with chopped herbs, serve with grated parmesan cheese.

Spaghetti Al Crudo
with Crispy Tilapia

Shared by Andrea Panno, Guilford

Andrea is one of the owners of The Guilford Bistro, formerly The Madison Bistro, as well as other restaurants in his hometown of Sicily, Italy. His unique style of cooking is sought after all along the shoreline.

3   large tomatoes, chopped
3   cloves garlic, crushed
    salt, to taste
    pepper, to taste
    parsley, to taste
2   tilapia filets
    flour

3   tablespoons water from pasta (for sauce)
2   tablespoons olive oil, for fish
1   pound spaghetti, cooked al dente
    arugula

Instructions:

Sauté tomatoes and garlic in olive oil for 1 minute. Add salt, pepper and parsley to taste. In a separate pan, fry tilapia that has been lightly dredged in flour until crispy. Set aside. Add precooked spaghetti in with tomato/garlic mixture, add more olive oil if needed and sauté for 1 minute. Add fresh arugula to tomato/garlic mixture, stir and plate. Top with crispy tilapia.

Fresh Herbed
Angel Hair Pasta

Shared by Merry Esposito, Madison

1	pound angel hair pasta	4	tablespoons fresh parsley, chopped
4	tablespoons olive oil		
1	teaspoons salt	4	teaspoons fresh basil, chopped
1/2	teaspoons fresh ground pepper	4	tablespoons Parmigiano-Reggiano, grated

Instructions:

Cook pasta according to directions, drain and return to pot. Add all the ingredients and toss. Keep warm until ready to serve. This is delicious with veal piccata, found on page 158.

Vodka Sauce

Shared by Margaret McNerney, Guilford

This is a great sauce, serve with a crisp salad and crusty bread!

1/3	pound bacon, diced	1/3	cup vodka
2	cups onions, chopped	1/2	cup green peas, fresh or frozen
1/4	teaspoon red pepper, crushed	1	cup heavy cream
2	tablespoons garlic, minced	1/4	cup fresh basil, chopped
1	14-ounce can tomatoes, crushed		

Instructions:

In a large skillet, cook bacon over medium high heat until fat is rendered and beginning to brown, about 4 minutes. Add onions and crushed red pepper, sauté until soft, about 6 minutes. Add garlic, cook for 1 minute. Add crushed tomatoes, stir to combine, and cook for 2 minutes. Add the vodka, cook until slightly reduced, add peas and cream, simmer until thickened, for about 2 minutes. Remove from heat and stir in basil. Serve immediately over your favorite pasta!

Chef Lou's Fettuccine

Shared by Chef Lou Castahno of Pasta Vita, Old Saybrook

$^1/_4$ cup olive oil

$1^1/_2$ pounds portobello
mushrooms, sliced

3 cloves garlic, sliced thin

3 ounces sun dried tomatoes,
sliced thin

1 bunch swiss chard

2 ounces white wine
salt, to taste
pepper, to taste

1 pound mascarpone cheese

$^1/_4$ cup parmesan cheese

1 pound fettuccine
parsley, to garnish

Instructions:

Heat 4 quarts of water. While water is heating, in a large pan, heat olive oil and sauté mushrooms and garlic and cook until mushrooms are tender. Add sun-dried tomatoes and swiss chard and cook until wilted. Add white wine and season with salt and pepper. Add salt to 4 quarts of water and cook fettuccine. In a separate bowl, add mascarpone cheese and a bit of pasta water to incorporate. In a separate large mixing bowl, add cooked pasta, mascarpone cheese and parmesan cheese and mushroom mixture. Adjust seasonings, add some of the reserved pasta water if necessary and mix until combined. Serve immediately.

Bolognese Sauce

Shared by Margaret McNerney, Guilford

This is a crowd pleasing pasta sauce, used when entertaining family and friends. Everyone loves it!

1^1/$_2$ tablespoons butter	1 pound veal, ground
1^1/$_2$ tablespoons extra virgin olive oil	2 cups whole milk
1 large onion, diced	1 cup red wine
2 stalks celery, diced	1 14^1/$_2$-ounce can beef stock
4-5 baby carrots, diced	^{1}/$_2$ cup tomato paste
1 pound sirloin, ground	salt, to taste
	pepper, to taste

Instructions:

Heat butter and oil in large pot over medium heat. Add onions and cook until softened, about 5 minutes. Add celery and carrots, cook until vegetables are tender, 8–10 minutes. Add ground sirloin and veal. Cook until meat is no longer pink, stirring occasionally. Add milk, cook at a gentle simmer, skimming fat from surface, until liquid is reduced by half, approximately 50 minutes. Add wine, simmer until liquid is reduced by half again, another 40 minutes. Add beef stock, tomato paste, salt and pepper, simmer gently until sauce thickens, about 40–45 minutes. Serve over your favorite pasta! This makes 1^1/$_2$ quarts.

Spaghetti with Fresh Sardines

Shared by Andrea Panno of Guilford

1   medium red onion, chopped

3   tablespoons olive oil

1   pound fresh sardines

$^{1}/_{2}$ cup white wine

1   tablespoon pignoli nuts

1   tablespoon raisins
    handful fresh wild fennel,
    chopped

1   cup tomato sauce

    salt, to taste

    pepper, to taste

1   cup sugar

1   cup bread crumbs

1   pound spaghetti, cooked
    al dente

Instructions:

Sauté red onion over medium heat, until soft in olive oil. Add sardines and cook 1 minute on each side. Add white wine and simmer for 4–5 minutes. Add pignoli nuts, raisins, wild fennel and 1 cup of tomato sauce. Season with salt and pepper and simmer for 15 minutes.

In a separate pan, sauté bread crumbs and sugar, stirring continuously to prevent sugar from sticking, until browned. Cook pasta according to package instructions, coat with sardine sauce and sprinkle bread crumbs on top and serve!

Baked Salmon with Saffron

Shared by Edd's Place, Westbrook

$1/2$	filet of salmon	$1/2$	teaspoon sea salt
1	teaspoon saffron	$1/4$	teaspoon tumeric
1	teaspoon granulated garlic	12	ounces orange soda
$1/2$	teaspoon black pepper		

Instructions:

Spray sheet pan with non stick cooking spray. Place salmon on sheet and sprinkle with saffron. Sprinkle garlic, pepper, salt and tumaric on top of salmon. Gently pour orange soda over filet, the bottom of the sheet pan should be covered with the soda. Spray top of filet with vegetable spray and bake for 15 minutes in a 400 degree oven.

This recipe serves 8.

Shrimp, It's Hot, Hot, Hot!

Shared by Merry Esposito, Madison

This is our favorite family recipe. I recreated it from a dish that I first enjoyed at a restaurant in Newport, RI. The shrimp can be replaced with chicken and you can make the sauce as hot or as mild as you like.

1	quart lite cream	1	pound raw shrimp, peeled and de-veined
1	cup Pete's hot sauce		
1	pound rigatoni pasta	1	cup Parmigiano-Reggiano, shaved
1	14.5 ounce can of diced tomatoes with garlic		salt, to taste
3	cups baby spinach leaves		pepper, to taste

Instructions:

In a medium heavy pan, on medium low heat, gradually pour cream and hot sauce, stirring constantly until the sauce becomes thick and creamy. Be careful not to boil! Meanwhile, cook the rigatoni according to package directions. Add canned tomatoes to cream sauce and $2^1/2$ cups of the baby spinach. Keep this mixture warm on low heat. Season shrimp with salt and in a small skillet, quickly stir fry on high heat, just until the shrimp turns pink. Add the shrimp to the cream sauce and serve immediately over the pasta. Garnish with parmesan cheese and the remaining baby spinach leaves chopped.

Cliff's Chicken Rigatoni

Shared by Esther Magee, Madison

*When I grew up in Ithica, NY Italian cooking was superb!
This dish creates a stir every time I make it.*

1 whole chicken	3 ounces brandy
¹/₂ cup butter, melted	1 can whole peeled tomatoes
¹/₄ cup olive oil	1 pound rigatoni cooked according to package instructions
1 large onion, chopped	
1 16-ounce jar cherry peppers, seeded with juice	

Instructions:

Drizzle chicken with butter and olive oil. Bake at 350 degrees for one hour. Remove chicken, cool, de-bone and cut into chunks. Save drippings from chicken. In a large fry pan, sauté onion with peppers and their juice. When onions are partially cooked, add chicken drippings and continue cooking until onions are soft. Add chicken chunks and brandy, boil for 1–2 minutes to evaporate the alcohol. Crush the tomatoes and add to pan. Simmer sauce for 1 hour and pour over cooked rigatoni.

Garlic Shrimp with Plum Tomatoes and Pesto over Pappardelle

Shared by Diane Gardner, Madison

I made this up one night when I was looking for something quick and easy. It has become a favorite for my family! Prep all of your ingredients before you start and this is a 15 minute dish!

2 tablespoons butter	1/4 cup Parmigiano-Reggiano finely grated
2 tablespoons olive oil	
5-6 large garlic cloves, chopped	1 8.8-ounce package pappardelle pasta
8 jumbo shrimp, peeled, cut in half	
	2-3 tablespoons pesto
1 28-ounce can plum tomatoes heaping hand fresh basil, rolled and chopped	salt, to taste
	pepper, to taste

Instructions:

In a large fry pan, melt butter with olive oil and sauté garlic for 1–2 minutes, while garlic is still white and firm; add shrimp and toss for 1–2 minutes, leaving it slightly undercooked. Remove shrimp from pan and set aside. With your hands, take the plum tomatoes and squeeze into fry pan. Do not use the extra juice in can, tomatoes only, they will be in pieces. Let tomato sauté for about 3–4 minutes, and add shrimp back into the mixture. Turn off heat and add salt and pepper to taste, sprinkle with half of parmesan cheese.

Meanwhile, cook the pappardelle al dente, and transfer cooked pasta into fry pan with shrimp sauce. Do not drain pasta, use tongs and put directly into fry pan from boiling water. Turn stove back to medium heat and add pesto, toss gently as pasta dish is heating. Top with remaining cheese and serve immediately.

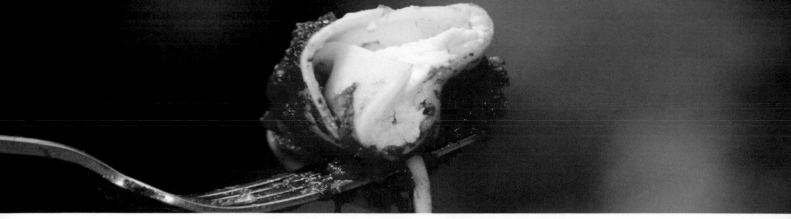

Baked Stuffed Manicotti

Shared by Cheryl Cianfaglione, Madison

This is my mother Hilda Ceragioli's recipe that she has been making for many years for my father, my husband Rick, myself and for our 3 boys.

Sauce:

3	tablespoons olive oil
1	medium onion, chopped
2	cloves garlic, chopped
1	large can tomato puree (rinse can out with water to achieve desired consistency)
1	tablespoon Italian seasoning
1	tablespoon parsley, dried
1	tablespoon sugar
	salt, to taste
	pepper, to taste

Filling:

1	package manicotti shells
1	16-ounce container ricotta cheese
2	eggs, beaten
2	tablespoons parsley, dried
1	teaspoon nutmeg
	salt, to taste
	pepper, to taste
	parmesan cheese, for topping

Instructions:

To make the sauce, brown together olive oil, onion and garlic in a heavy skillet over medium heat. Add remaining ingredients, cook for 1¹/₂ hours on medium heat.

Boil manicotti for 10 minutes, no more.

Meanwhile, combine all of the filling ingredients in a bowl. Drain manicotti and stuff with cheese filling. Coat bottom of casserole dish with sauce and line manicotti on top of sauce. Arrange all manicotti in one layer, top with more sauce. Sprinkle with parmesan cheese and cover with foil. Bake for 45 minutes in a 350 degree oven.

Cioppino

Shared by Star Fish Market, Guilford
A wonderful fish market that carries an amazing array of fresh fish!

$\star$

$^1/_3$ cup olive oil	1 cup fish stock
1 tablespoon butter	1 tablespoon tomato paste
3 garlic cloves, chopped	2 pounds little neck clams
1 medium onion, thinly sliced	1 pound monk fish, cut into 1 inch thick pieces (may substitute any white fish with 1 inch thickness, be sure to remove skin and bones)
1 jalapeño pepper, chopped fine	
1 small red pepper, chopped	
1 small green pepper, chopped	
2 stalks celery, chopped	1 pound shrimp, medium, peeled and deveined
$^1/_2$ teaspoon red pepper flakes	
$^1/_2$ teaspoon lemon grass	$^1/_2$ pound crab meat, picked (either all leg or jumbo lump)
2 28-ounce cans tomatoes, crushed	
$^1/_2$ cup red wine	1 pound mussels
1 teaspoon oregano, fresh, chopped	$^1/_4$ cup parsley, fresh, chopped
1 tablespoon basil, fresh, chopped	salt, to taste
$^1/_4$ cup cilantro, fresh, chopped	pepper, to taste

Instructions:

In a dutch oven, heat olive oil and butter over medium heat. Add garlic and onion and sauté until soft. Add peppers, celery, pepper flakes and lemon grass and sauté for 20 minutes. Stir in crushed tomatoes, wine, oregano, basil, cilantro, fish stock and tomato paste. Adjust with salt and pepper if needed. Add little neck clams and simmer for five minutes. Add monk fish and shrimp and let simmer for another five minutes. Add crab meat and mussels and continue simmering for three minutes. Remove dutch oven from stove, let sit for thirty minutes. Ladle broth and fish together into six large bowls, top with parsley and salt and pepper to taste.

Sesame Crusted Salmon
with Spicy Spinach

Shared by The Cooking Company, Killingworth

¹/₄	cup bread crumbs	2	tablespoons paprika
¹/₂	cup sesame seeds	¹/₄	cup toasted sesame oil
	salt, to taste	2	pounds skinless salmon filets
	pepper, to taste	2	tablespoons canola oil

Instructions:

Preheat oven to 350 degrees. In a bowl, combine bread crumbs, sesame seeds, salt, pepper, paprika and sesame oil. Press the salmon filets flesh side down, into this bread crumb mixture and coat well. Place a sauté pan over medium high heat and add the canola oil. Place the breaded salmon, crumb side down, in the hot pan and sear for 1–2 minutes or until evenly browned. Place the fish on a baking pan and bake for 10 minutes or until cooked to desired doneness. See Spicy Spinach on page 96.

Super Salmon Cakes

Shared by Monica Pitney, East Haddam

This recipe lets the flavor of the salmon shine—not the bread crumbs. It's been changed a little bit over the years. Now I think it's just about perfect!

1	large potato, cooked and slightly mashed	4	tablespoons milk
1	7$^{1}/_{2}$-ounce can wild salmon, drained	1	tablespoon prepared mustard
$^{1}/_{2}$	cup Panko bread crumbs	1	tablespoon mayonnaise
4	ounces salmon, smoked	1$^{1}/_{2}$	tablespoons capers, chopped
		2	tablespoons fresh dill, chopped

Instructions:

In a large bowl, combine all ingredients until completely blended. Form 6 oval patties and cook in a sauté pan over medium heat for 5 minutes on each side. These are especially tasty when served with Robert Rothschild's lemon, dill and capers sauce!

Mussels in White Clam Sauce

Shared by Liz Wallack, Madison

¹/₄ stick butter

3 tablespoons olive oil

3-4 cloves fresh garlic, chopped

3 pound mussels, washed

1 15-ounce can white clam pasta sauce

1 cup white wine

10 pieces sun dried tomatoes, chopped

1 small bunch fresh rosemary, chopped

1 small bunch fresh cilantro, chopped

crushed red pepper, to taste

juice of 1 lemon

¹/₄ cup parmesan cheese

Instructions:

In a large heavy skillet, over medium heat, warm the butter and olive oil, add the garlic and saute until lightly browned. Add mussels to the pan and then add the white clam pasta sauce and white wine. Let this cook for 5 minutes then add the sun dried tomatoes, herbs, salt and pepper and lemon juice. When mussels have opened, transfer to a plate and top with parmesan cheese. Serve immediately!

Baked Tilapia with Sourdough Bread Crumbs, Bacon and Herbs

Shared by Robert's Food Center, Madison

A favorite of Robert's customers!

2	tilapia filets, approximately 4-6 ounces each	1	teaspoon fresh thyme, chopped
1/8	teaspoon Old Bay Seasoning	1	teaspoon fresh oregano, chopped
1 1/2	cups sourdough bread crumbs (use day old sourdough bread and rough chop in food processor)	1	tablespoon romano cheese, freshly grated
2	slices bacon, cooked crisp and crumbled	1/8	teaspoon black pepper, ground
1	teaspoon fresh parsley, chopped		enough garlic oil to make a mixture that will bind ingredients together

Instructions:

Preheat oven to 410 degrees and spray a baking dish with non stick olive oil cooking spray. Season tilapia filets with Old Bay Seasoning. In a small bowl, combine all remaining ingredients adding enough garlic oil to bind the ingredients together. Pat half of this mixture onto the top of each filet. Bake for 20 minutes or until an internal temperature of 155 degrees is reached. Enjoy!

Baked Flounder with Shallots, Tomato and Mozzarella

Shared by Robert's Food Center, Madison

This is a dish that we prepare about twice a month in our food court, it's a specialty that our customers look forward to.

✳

4	flounder filets, approximately 2 ounces each	4	slices fresh tomato, cut into $1/8$ inch thick slices
1	shallot, diced fine	$1/2$	cup mozzarella cheese, shredded
1	teaspoon parsley, freshly chopped		salt, to taste
			pepper, to taste
$1/8$	teaspoon Old Bay Seasoning	2	ounces white wine

Instructions:

Preheat oven to 400 degrees. Form two portions of flounder by stacking two filets on top of one another, tuck tails under for uniform thickness. Sprinkle each portion with shallot, parsley and Old Bay Seasoning. Top with tomato slices, sprinkle cheese on top of tomato, and salt and pepper. Place flounder stacks in a casserole, pour wine in bottom of casserole and bake for 20–25 minutes or until an internal thermometer reaches 155 degrees.

Seafood Casserole

Shared by Valerie Engstrom, Branford

I first enjoyed this at the Wallingford VNA holiday party many years ago!

✳

1	tablespoon Worcestershire sauce	1	package frozen shrimp (1.5 oz)
	pinch garlic salt	1	package crab meat (canned or frozen)
1	cup cream of shrimp soup	1	large container lobster (found in refrigerated area of supermarket)
2	cups mayonnaise		
$1^{1}/2$	cups green or red peppers, diced		
$1^{1}/2$	cups celery, chopped	$1/2$	cup Italian style bread crumbs
$2/3$	cup onion, chopped	2	tablespoons butter

Instructions:

In a large baking dish, combine all ingredients. Cover top with bread crumbs and dot with butter. Bake at 350 degrees, uncovered for 40 minutes.

Baked Black Cod

Shared by Mike & Colette Lukas, Star Fish Market, Guilford

I	shallot, thinly sliced	1	sprig rosemary, chopped
1/2	cup cherry tomatoes	1	lime, juiced
1	tablespoon extra virgin olive oil	1	pound fresh black cod or sable lime zest, to taste
1/3	cup basil, chopped		

Instructions:

Pre-heat oven to 400 degrees. Let cod reach room temperature while sautéing ingredients. Heat olive oil in medium sauce pan, add shallot and cherry tomatoes, let simmer for 5 minutes. Lightly oil a shallow baking dish or sheet pan. On flesh side of cod, add light coating of oil along with basil and rosemary. Squeeze small wedges of lime over fish.

Cook cod for 15 minutes at 400 degrees. Continue to simmer shallots and tomatoes while cod is baking. Pour shallots and tomatoes over top of fish and finish with salt, pepper and lime zest.

Sea Scallops with Apple Smoked Bacon & Wild Mushroom Ragout

Shared by Zandra Baker, Palmer's Market, Darien

12 jumbo sea scallops
12 pieces apple wood smoked bacon
2 large portabello mushrooms, sliced
4 medium sized crimini mushrooms, sliced
6 medium sized white button mushrooms, sliced
4 tablespoons olive oil, divided
1 small bunch of fresh thyme, chopped
2 cloves garlic, minced
1 can black eyed peas
   salt, to taste
   pepper, to taste

Instructions:

Remove mussel from each of the scallops, rinse and pat dry with a paper towel. Wrap each scallop with one strip of bacon and secure each with 2 toothpicks. Season scallops with salt and pepper, place on a sheet pan and set aside. Place all sliced mushrooms in a bowl and set aside. Heat large sauté pan and pour 2 tablespoons of olive oil into pan. When pan is very hot, sear the scallops on each side until golden brown. Place scallops back on sheet pan and cook in a 350 degree oven for 5 minutes. Add remaining 2 tablespoons olive oil to sauté pan, place mushrooms, thyme, garlic and black eyed peas in pan and sauté until mushrooms are tender. Place a spoonful of this ragout in the center of a plate, remove toothpicks from scallops and surround ragout with 3 scallops per plate.

Sicilian Supper

Shared by Susan Miller, Madison

2	pounds ground beef	1	package egg noodles
1	cup onion, chopped	2	8-ounce packages cream cheese
	salt, to taste		
	pepper, to taste	$1^1/_2$ cups whole milk	
2	6-ounce cans tomato paste	1	cup parmesan cheese, grated
12	ounces water (I refill the empty tomato paste cans)	1	teaspoon garlic powder
		1	cup green pepper, chopped

Instructions:

In a large heavy skillet, fry beef, onion, and season with salt and pepper. Add tomato paste and water and simmer for 10 minutes. Cook egg noodles according to package instructions. In another skillet, over low heat, melt cream cheese, milk, parmesan cheese, garlic powder and green pepper. Combine cooked noodles and cheese sauce. In a 9 x 13 baking dish, alternate layers of meat sauce and noodle cheese mixture. Start and end with meat sauce. Sprinkle additional parmesan cheese on top and bake for 30–45 minutes at 350 degrees. Cut into squares and serve like lasagna.

Thompson's Baked Swordfish

Shared by Bill Carroll, New York

Growing up in Connecticut and spending every summer on Cape Cod was quite a privilege! My annual summer job, and that of hundreds of other high school and college kids, was working at Thompson's Clam Bar in Harwichport. Although Thompson's is no longer there, this recipe reminds me of the years I spent having fun in and out of the kitchen!

2 swordfish filets, cut thick, at least 1 1/2 inches	1/4 teaspoon salt
2 heaping tablespoons Hellman's mayonnaise	1/4 teaspoon celery salt
1 cup Ritz crackers, crushed	1/4 teaspoon black pepper, freshly ground
	paprika

Instructions:

Rinse filets clean and pat dry with a paper towel. Completely coat both sides of each filet with mayonnaise. Spread crushed Ritz crackers on a paper plate and press each filet into crackers on both sides. Use your hands to make sure the crackers are really sticking well to the mayonnaise. Place filets in a casserole sprayed with non stick cooking spray. Generously sprinkle each filet with salt, celery salt and pepper. Bake swordfish in a 400 degree oven, uncovered, for 20–30 minutes or until completely cooked through. Remove from oven and sprinkle with paprika for color.

Scallops on Spinach
with Apple Brandy Sauce

Shared by Vilma Roetting Cook, Madison

This is one of my husbands' Captain Bud Cook's, favorite recipes when sailing aboard the Rum Runner 3!

1¹/₂	teaspoons olive oil		salt, to taste
1	shallot, minced		pepper, to taste
¹/₃	cup Calvados brandy	¹/₂	cup apple juice
1	cup heavy whipping cream	1	teaspoon fresh thyme, chopped
12	sea scallops	1	garlic clove, minced
¹/₂	teaspoon vegetable oil	1	9-ounce bag spinach, fresh

Instructions:

In a large non stick skillet, heat ¹/₂ teaspoon olive oil over medium high heat. Add shallot and stir for 30 seconds. Add Calvados and boil for 30 seconds, brandy may ignite. Add cream and boil for 2 minutes, transfer sauce to a bowl. Sprinkle scallops with salt and pepper. Heat vegetable oil over high heat in a large skillet. Add scallops and cook until brown, about 2 minutes per side. Transfer scallops to rimmed baking sheet and place in oven to keep warm. Add apple juice and thyme to hot skillet. Boil 1 minute, scraping up brown bits. Add reserved brandy sauce to skillet, bring to a boil and then remove from heat. Cook spinach in 1 tablespoon olive oil for 2 minutes. Mound spinach on 2 plates, top with scallops and sauce.

Lazy Lobster

Shared by Beth Garbo, Stonington

This is a great recipe for leftover lobster meat. You can put it in a hot dog roll or eat it right out of the pan like an authentic Italian fisherman!

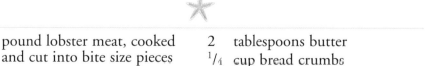

1	pound lobster meat, cooked and cut into bite size pieces	2	tablespoons butter
		¹/₄	cup bread crumbs

Instructions:

In a large heavy sauce pan, melt butter over medium heat. Put lobster into butter and toss to coat with butter. Add bread crumbs and cook just until moist and lobster is warmed through.

Fish with Grapes

Shared by Cassy Pickard, Guilford

2	tablespoons olive oil
1	large bunch red or black seedless grapes, cut in half, lengthwise
$^1/_4$-$^1/_2$	pound thick white fish per person (halibut, cod or any favorite fish)
	salt, to taste
	pepper, to taste
$^1/_4$	cup marsala wine, port or something similar

Instructions:

In a large heavy skillet, on medium heat, pour one tablespoon olive oil and heat until oil begins to sizzle. Place grapes cut side down, adjust the heat so that the grapes don't burn. Resist the temptation to move the grapes around, as the goal is to let them sit and caramelize to a golden brown. Once the grapes look ready, carefully scrape them to the sides of the skillet. Season both sides of the fish with salt and pepper. Heat 1 tablespoon oil in center of skillet. When the oil is glistening, add the fish. Let the fish cook undisturbed until you see the color beginning to change up the side of the fish. If you are using a thin fish, such as flounder, you'll have to decide when to flip it. Carefully flip the fish and brown the other side. The fish is done when it is slightly flaky when touched with a fork. Use your judgment so that the fish is neither over or under cooked. Transfer the fish to a warmed plate. Pour wine into skillet to deglaze the pan, gently incorporating the grapes. Taste the sauce and adjust the seasoning. Pour sauce over the fish, arranging the grapes in an artful way!

The trick to this super, simple recipe is not to stir the food too often, so that the grapes can caramelize and the fish won't fall apart. This recipe can be altered to suit the number of people being served, go with your own judgment when preparing it. You can use any white fish, a thinner fish tends to fall apart when cooking but, certainly could be carefully used. Don't be put off by the lengthy instructions, this is one of the easiest recipes I enjoy making!

Tilapia Medeterrani

Shared by Andrea Panno, Guilford Bistro and Grill, Guilford

4	tilapia filets	1	cup fresh tomato filets
	flour	1/2	cup clam juice
2	teaspoons butter	12	asparagus spears
2	teaspoons olive oil		salt, to taste
1/2	cup white wine		pepper, to taste
	sherry, splash		parsley, to taste

Instructions:

Flour both sides of filets and sauté in preheated pan with olive oil and butter over medium heat. Next, add white wine and a splash of sherry. Add tomato filets. Season with fresh parsley, salt and pepper to taste. Add clam juice and cook for 10 minutes over low heat. Add asparagus and cook for another 2 minutes and serve immediately.

hearty dinners

Chicken from the Hall

Champagne Chicken

Meatloaf with Spinach and Swiss Cheese

Holiday Brisket

Grilled NY Strip Steak with Chimichuri Sauce

Eggplant Parmigiana

Chicken and Dumplings

Holiday Ham with Mustard, Molasses Glaze

Mattie's Favorite Pot Roast

Perfect Party Steaks

Osso Bucco

Coca Cola Brisket

Tuscan Short Ribs

French Canadian Meat Pie

Chicken and Prosciutto Roll-ups

Dot's Beef Burgundy

Veal Piccata

Pork Tenderloin in Black Truffle Sauce

Beef Stroganoff

Millionaire's Chow Mein

Flank Steak with Tomatoes

on the lighter side

Not Your Mama's Grilled Cheese

Thanksgiving Wrap

Kristen's Mushroom Burger

Chicken from the Hall

Shared by Sherry Casagranda, Groton

My father-in-law, Mr. Casagranda, spent a lot of time at the Italian-American Hall in New London. This is one of the recipes from the Hall that is a especially cherished since the Hall is no longer there.

✶

$^1/_2$ teaspoon salt	$^1/_2$ cup butter
$^1/_2$ teaspoon pepper	$^1/_2$ cup canola oil
4 cloves garlic, chopped	8 ounces red wine, may use white wine
2 tablespoons rosemary, chopped	
3 pounds chicken breasts with bones	1 8-ounce can chopped tomatoes
	1 small sweet onion, sliced

Instructions:

In a large bowl combine salt, pepper, garlic and rosemary, add chicken (with skin) to the bowl and mix well. Cover bowl and refrigerate overnight. In a large skillet, heat butter and oil, quickly sauté onions. Add wine and tomatoes, cook for 5 minutes on medium heat. Put marinated chicken in a roasting pan, skin sides up. Pour the butter/tomato mixture over chicken and bake for 40 minutes in a 350 degree oven or until chicken is cooked through and browned.

Champagne Chicken

Shared by Amy Vrzal, Stamford

✶

4 tablespoons butter	1 cup champagne
2 skinless chicken breasts, sliced thin	$^1/_2$ cup heavy cream
4 tablespoons shallots, chopped	$^1/_4$ teaspoon salt

Instructions:

In a large skillet over medium high heat, warm 2 tablespoons butter. Add chicken and cook for three minutes per side until golden. Remove the chicken to a warmed plate. Add 1 tablespoon butter to pan along with shallots and cook until translucent. Add the champagne and cook until it is reduced by half. Add the cream and chicken back into the pan, salt to taste. Sauté just until the sauce thickens. Just before serving, whisk in remaining 1 tablespoon butter and serve warm.

This recipe serves 4.

Meat Loaf with Spinach and Swiss Cheese

Shared by Joy Scott, Guilford

1¹/₂ pounds ground beef
¹/₂ cup bread crumbs
2 eggs, beaten
¹/₄ cup light soy sauce
¹/₄ teaspoon salt

¹/₄ teaspoon pepper
1 package fresh spinach, washed, stems removed
1 cup light swiss cheese, shredded

Instructions:

In a large bowl, combine ground beef with bread crumbs, eggs, soy sauce, salt and pepper. Form beef mixture into an oblong shape and stuff spinach and cheese into the middle. This can be prepared the night before and you may substitute any other green vegetable or any other cheese.

Bake for 35-45 minutes in a 350 degree oven.

Holiday Brisket

Shared by Marlene Yahalom, New York , New York

This is a great holiday favorite, especially for families of Eastern European origin. Preparation can be simple or flavored with more than a dozen different ingredients. For maximum tenderness, slice the meat against the grain. This is best prepared one day ahead and served with horseradish!

2	12 ounce bottles dark beer	1	teaspoon black pepper
2	cups whole berry cranberry sauce	1	teaspoon paprika
1/2	cup ketchup	8	teaspoons olive oil
1/4	cup all purpose flour	1	5-pound brisket, first cut
1	teaspoon sea salt	7	medium white onions, sliced into rings
	dash of red pepper		horseradish

Instructions:

In a medium sized bowl, combine beer, cranberry sauce, ketchup and flour. In a separate bowl combine salt, peppers, paprika and 3 teaspoons olive oil. Brush both sides of brisket with seasoning/oil mixture. Pour 3 teaspoons of olive oil into the bottom of a 6 quart dutch oven or pot. Heat oil over high heat, place brisket into pot and brown approximately 10 minutes on each side. When browned, remove brisket from pot. In a separate pan, heat remaining 2 teaspoons oil and add onions, sautéing for approximately 7 minutes until brown and tender. Stir frequently so that the onions don't stick to the bottom of the pan. Line sautéed onions in the bottom of the dutch oven/pot, top with brisket, pour beer mixture over brisket. Bake covered for 3 hours on 350 degrees, then cool for 1/2 an hour. Remove brisket from gravy and refrigerate both separately overnight. The next day, slice meat against the grain, remove fat from top of gravy. Reheat both the sliced meat and gravy on low heat so that the meat can absorb the flavors.

Grilled NY Strip Steak with Chimichuri Sauce

Shared by Zandra Baker, Palmer's Market, Darien
This is a wonderful dinner served with Palmer's Traditional Steak Fries.

1	bunch parsley	$^1/_4$	cup honey
1	bunch cilantro	4	8-ounce New York strip steaks
6	cloves garlic		salt, to taste
$^1/_4$	cup lime juice		pepper, to taste
$^1/_4$	cup red wine vinegar		

Instructions:

In a food processor, place the parsley, cilantro, and garlic, pulse 3-4 times, until chopped. Add the lime juice, red wine vinegar and honey and pulse until well combined. Set this chimichuri sauce aside. Season steaks with salt and pepper and grill until desired doneness. Ladle chimichuri sauce on top of steak and serve immediately! Serve with Palmer's Traditional Steak Fries. See recipe on page 88.

This recipe serves 4.

Eggplant Parmigiana

Shared by Saldamarco's, Clinton

2	large eggplants peeled and sliced into $1/4$ inch thick slices	1	cup tomato sauce
1	cup flour	$1/2$	cup parmesan cheese, grated
2	eggs, beaten		salt, to taste
	vegetable oil, for frying		pepper, to taste

Instructions:

Season flour with salt and pepper. Dredge sliced eggplant in flour and shake off excess. Dip in egg until well coated on both sides. Heat vegetable oil in a large skillet until very hot. Fry on one side and flip to the other when the first side is lightly browned. Drain each piece of eggplant, completely on paper towels. Coat bottom of a baking dish with tomato sauce and layer eggplant in bottom. Top with sauce and sprinkle generously with grated cheese. Continue this process until eggplant reaches the brim of the pan, finish with sauce and cheese. Bake covered for 45 minutes to an hour in a 350 degree oven. Remove cover and place under broiler for 2 minutes to brown the top. Let cool for 5 minutes before serving.

Chicken and Dumplings

Shared by Fran Gardner, Florence, South Carolina

A long time friend of the Gardner family and an excellent cook!

1   3 pound chicken (chicken breast can be substituted)
1   teaspoon salt
$1/2$ teaspoon pepper
2   stalks celery, chopped
1   small onion, chopped
2   chicken bouillon cubes
    water
1   can cream of celery soup

Dumplings:

2   cups all purpose flour
1   teaspoon salt
$3/4$ cup ice cold water

Instructions:

Place chicken, salt, pepper, celery, onion and bouillon cubes in a large cooking pot. Fill with enough water to completely cover the chicken. Bring to a boil and continue boiling until chicken falls off the bones. Remove chicken from water and pull remaining meat off the bones. Return chicken pieces back to pot, add cream of celery soup and bring to a boil.

To make dumplings, place flour in mixing bowl and stir with salt, making sure that the salt is evenly distributed. Pour a small amount of ice water into flour and blend it. Continue adding the water until all flour is mixed in. If the dough seems too sticky to handle, add a little more flour. Coat your hands and rolling pin with flour. Take a small amount of flour mixture and roll into an oblong circle, cut the circle into strips about 1-2 inches long. Place these on wax paper that has been dusted with flour. Continue working with the wet dough bit by bit until it has all been used. Drop 1 dough strip at a time into boiling chicken stock. Reduce heat to simmer, cover pot and cook dumplings for 30-45 minutes. Do not stir, shake the pot to mix dumplings. If the broth seems too thin, combine 2 tablespoons cornstarch with $1/4$ cup water to thicken.

Holiday Ham with Mustard, Molasses Glaze

Shared by Mark Castaldo, Madison
We eat ham once a year in our house on Christmas day!

3/4	cup Gulden's spicy brown mustard	1/2	teaspoon cloves, ground
1/4	cup light molasses	1	8-pound ham, fully cooked
1/4	cup honey	1 1/2	cups Ritz crackers, crushed

Instructions:

In a small bowl stir together mustard, molasses, honey and cloves. Trim rind and excess fat from ham and score top of ham. Place ham in roasting pan and brush top with 1/2 of mustard mixture. Bake uncovered for 15 minutes in a 350 degree oven. Remove ham from oven and cover loosely with tin foil, bake for another 30 minutes. Remove ham from oven and coat with remaining mustard glaze, press Ritz crackers onto glaze. Turn oven up to 425 degrees and place ham back in oven uncovered for 20 minutes, until crackers are golden. Transfer ham to platter and serve warm.

Mattie's Favorite Pot Roast

Shared by Amy Woodford, Old Saybrook

1	2-3 pound rump roast		pinch of thyme, dried
1/4	cup flour		pinch of marjoram, dried
1	teaspoon salt	2	large onions, sliced
1	teaspoon pepper	8	medium carrots, quartered
2-4	tablespoons olive oil	6	stalks celery, sliced
4	cloves garlic, chopped	2	cups dry red wine
1/3	cup brandy	2	cups hot water
3	bay leaves		

Instructions:

Dredge roast in flour seasoned with salt and pepper. In a heavy skillet on medium heat, heat oil and garlic, place roast in skillet and brown on all sides. Remove roast from heat and pour brandy into skillet. Flames will shoot up so be careful! When flames have gone out, transfer roast to large casserole, add spices and vegetables. Add wine to drippings in skillet and bring to a boil. Scrape sides and bottom of skillet, pour skillet drippings over roast in casserole. Pour hot water over casserole, cover and cook for 4 hours on 350 degrees. When done, slice roast and serve on a large platter, with vegetables on the side.

Perfect Party Steaks

Shared by Diane Ifkovic, Guilford

This is a great recipe and perfect for a dinner party, as most of the work is done the night before!

8	1-inch thick beef filets, 6-8 ounces each	$2^1/_2$	teaspoons tomato paste
$2^1/_2$	garlic cloves, minced	$^3/_4$-1	cup dry red wine
$^1/_2$	teaspoon salt	1	cup chicken broth
$^1/_2$	teaspoon pepper	$^1/_2$	cup beef broth
1	tablespoon butter, plus $^1/_2$ stick	$^1/_4$	teaspoon Worcestershire sauce
3	tablespoons brandy	$2^1/_2$	tablespoons current jelly
4	tablespoons flour	$^1/_2$	pound mushrooms, sliced

Instructions:

Make a paste of garlic, salt and pepper and rub on both sides of steaks. Heat 1 tablespoon butter in large skillet until very hot. Sauté meat until brown on both sides, but still rare in the center. Place steaks in casserole, do not crowd.

Add brandy to skillet and cook over moderate heat, stirring constantly and scraping bottom of pan. Add the $^1/_2$ stick of butter and when melted and foaming stir in flour and reduce heat. Whisk until golden brown and add tomato paste and rest of garlic. Mixture will be thick. Whisk in wine and broth and bring to a boil. Simmer for 10 minutes or reduce by $^1/_3$. Whisk in Worcestershire sauce and jelly and cook until jelly melts. Add mushrooms. Adjust seasonings and add more wine if mixture is too thick. Cool completely and pour over steaks. Cover and refrigerate overnight.

Bring to room temperature and preheat oven to 400 degrees. Bake uncovered for 15–20 minutes for medium rare. Spoon sauce over steaks when serving.

Osso Bucco

Shared by Sue Zaccagnino, Madison

1	cup flour	3	tablespoons tomato paste
1/2	teaspoon salt	3/4	cup canned brown gravy
1/2	teaspoon pepper	1	teaspoon oregano, dried
8	veal shanks, 2 inches thick	2	bay leaves, chopped
2	tablespoons corn oil	1/4	teaspoon thyme, dried
1	large onion, chopped	1	teaspoon Worcestershire sauce
4	cloves garlic, sliced paper thin	1/2	teaspoon Tabasco sauce
1	cup dry white wine		
1	28 ounce can peeled and chopped tomatoes		

Instructions:

Mix flour with salt and pepper over medium heat and dredge both sides of veal shanks in flour. Heat oil in Dutch oven, sauté veal on all sides until browned, approximately 4-5 minutes per side. Add onion and garlic to dutch oven and cook for 3-4 minutes. Add wine and cook for 3-4 minutes, add tomato paste and brown gravy, continue cooking. Stir in remaining seasonings and sauces. Remove from heat, cover and cook for 2 hours and 20 minutes in a 350 degree oven. Remove veal from Dutch oven and cook sauce on high heat for 2-3 minutes. Pour sauce over veal and serve. *Enjoy!*

Coca Cola Brisket

Shared by Lee White, Old Lyme
*This recipe has been adapted and with special thanks
to Eunice Schaub of Stonington.*

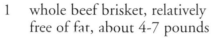

1	whole beef brisket, relatively free of fat, about 4-7 pounds	2	envelopes Lipton onion soup mix
1	large Vidalia onion, thickly sliced	1	12 ounce bottle Heinz chili sauce
16	ounces mushrooms, sliced	1	12 ounce can Coca Cola, not diet

Instructions:

Preheat oven to 350 degrees. Line a large roasting pan with enough heavy duty aluminum foil to cover the entire roast. Place brisket in center of foil and sprinkle onions and mushrooms on top of brisket. Shake contents of onion soup mix packets on top of brisket. Pour chili sauce over soup mix and then pour Coca Cola over that. Completely tent the brisket with foil and bake in oven for at least 4 hours. Remove brisket from pan and place on a cutting board, cover with aluminum foil to keep moist. Place roasting pan on top of cook top with juice and veggies in the pan. If the roasting pan can not be used on a cook top, pour juices and veggies into another pan. Heat juices and veggies on medium high heat, uncovered for 10–15 minutes until reduced. Slice brisket and pour syrupy juice and veggies over it. Serve immediately.

Tuscan Short Ribs

Shared by Chef Lou Castahno of Pasta Vita, Old Saybrook

⭐

5	pounds beef short ribs, trimmed of visible fat
	salt, to taste
	pepper, to taste
	all purpose flour, to dredge ribs
4	ounces olive oil, for searing, add more if needed
1	medium onion, diced small
1	small carrot, diced small
3	garlic cloves, lightly pounded
1	teaspoon sugar
2	ounces tomato paste
1	cup dry red wine, preferably from Tuscany
1	6-ounce can plum tomatoes, crushed
1	cup beef broth, low salt or fresh beef stock
1	bunch thyme, tied
1	bay leaf, dried or fresh
1/2	bunch parsley, chopped
1	handful porcini mushrooms, dried, soaked in hot water, then chopped
	a splash of juice from porcini mushrooms

Instructions:

Have butcher remove visible fat from ribs. Season ribs with salt and pepper, then dredge in flour. In a heavy skillet over medium high heat, sear ribs in 2 tablespoons olive oil until browned on all sides. Remove ribs from pan and set aside.

Drain oil from pan and add 2 tablespoons olive oil. Cook onions, carrots, garlic, add sugar and cook until lightly caramelized. Then add tomato paste and continue to cook until light brown (do not burn). Add red wine, plum tomatoes, beef broth, thyme, bay leaf, parsley, porcini mushrooms with a little of their liquid and salt and pepper. Bring to a boil, add short ribs and lower heat. Cover and cook approximately 1 1/2 hours or until very tender.

Lift meat out and skim off fat from sauce. Adjust seasoning. You can then strain the sauce and reduce until desired consistency or serve unstrained for a more Tuscan style. Serve with risotto, orzo or couscous.

French Canadian Meat Pie

Shared by John Carroll, formerly of Woodbridge

*This is a cherished recipe from my Memere who brought it with
her from Quebec to Claremont, New Hampshire as a young girl.
My family has enjoyed meat pie on Christmas Eve for as long
as I can remember. Since moving to California, I look forward
to coming back to New England at Christmas time to enjoy this
traditional meal. Some family members love meat pie more than
others, especially my brother, Billy, who always finds room in his
suitcase to bring leftovers back to New York City for his freezer!
This is especially good served with lots of cranberry sauce.*

4   large potatoes, peeled and quartered
2   cups water
$1^1/_2$ pounds ground pork
1   small onion, chopped
$^1/_2$ teaspoon cloves, ground
$^1/_2$ teaspoon cinnamon
$^1/_4$ teaspoon salt
$^1/_4$ teaspoon pepper

Pie crust:
2   cups flour
$^1/_2$ cup milk
$^1/_4$ cup oil
1   teaspoon salt

Instructions:

In a large pot, boil potatoes in 2 cups of water. When cooked through,
do not drain potatoes but rather, keep potatoes in pot and mash the potatoes into the water that they were boiled in. Add ground pork, onions
and seasonings to mashed potatoes and let cook covered for 3 hours on
low heat. Pour pork mixture into pie crust and top with second crust.
Make slits in top and bake at 370 degrees for one hour.

Pie Crust: Combine all ingredients with a fork. Make 2 crusts by rolling
dough out on floured surface between pieces of wax paper.

Chicken and Prosciutto Roll-ups

Shared by Ann Rowley, Old Saybrook

8-10	chicken breasts, very thinly sliced	1	cup chicken stock
8-10	slices prosciutto de parma, thinly sliced	2/3	cup cooking sherry
1/2	pound gruyere cheese, grated		olive oil
			salt, to taste
			pepper, to taste

Instructions:

In skillet, brown chicken breast in olive oil, adding salt and pepper to taste. Drain excess oil from chicken. Place 1 slice of prosciutto on chicken, top with 2 or 3 tablespoons of gruyere and gently roll chicken slices and secure with a toothpick.

Place rolled chicken on baking dish, add chicken stock and sherry. Cover and bake at 375 degrees for 20 minutes. Uncover and bake for another 10 minutes. *This recipes serves 4.*

Dot's Beef Burgundy

Shared by Dot Reiser, Mystic

2	pounds sirloin tips		salt to taste
1	can cream of mushroom soup		pepper, to taste
1/2	can beef broth	1	package egg noodles
1/2	can red wine, measure in soup can		

Instructions:

Put all ingredients into a casserole, except the egg noodles, cover and cook on 250 degrees for 5 hours. Cook egg noodles right before serving, spoon the beef burgundy over the noodles.

Veal Piccata

Shared by Mark Esposito, Madison

2	cups flour	1	cup white wine, dry
2	teaspoons salt	$^1/_2$	cup chicken stock
2	teaspoons pepper	4	tablespoons lemon juice, fresh
12	3-ounce veal medallions, cut into $^1/_4$ inch thick pieces	3	tablespoons capers
4	tablespoons olive oil	4	teaspoons garlic, minced
6	tablespoons butter, divided	2	teaspoons parsley, chopped

Instructions:

Combine flour with salt and pepper. Dredge both sides of each veal piece in flour. In a large heavy skillet, melt olive oil and butter over medium heat. Cook veal in batches until lightly browned, about $1^1/_2$–2 minutes per side. Remove veal from skillet and let drain on paper towels. Return skillet to heat and add wine, bring to a boil and let reduce by half. Add chicken stock, lemon juice, capers and garlic. Return this mixture to a boil and let boil until it gets thick. Stir in 4 tablespoons butter and 2 teaspoons parsley. Add veal pieces back to pan and cook for one more minute. Serve veal with angel hair pasta with fresh herbs on page 117.

Pork Tenderloin in Black Truffle Sauce

Shared by Bonnie Foster, Westbrook

1	pound pork tenderloin	1/4	cup white truffle oil
1	cup flour, seasoned with salt and pepper	1	cup light cream
		2	ounces black truffle paté*

Instructions:

Slice pork tenderloin into 1 inch thick pieces and pound with a mallet to thin out. Coat all sides with seasoned flour. In a large heavy skillet, heat truffle oil on medium heat, place tenderloin pieces into oil and brown for about 2 minutes per side. Remove tenderloin pieces from pan and set aside. Remove excess oil from pan, and in the same pan, add cream and paté. Whisk both on medium heat until thoroughly blended. Return pork pieces to sauce and let sauce reduce slightly. This is great served over risotto!

Black truffle paté can be purchased at Fromage Fine Foods & Coffees in Old Saybrook and other fine food specialty stores.

Beef Stroganoff

Shared by Walt's Market, Old Saybrook

Walt's Market was founded in 1960 by Walt Kozey. For the past 14 years it has been run by his son, Paul. Walt's serves wonderful homemade soups, salads and dinners and offers some of the best cuts of meat on the shoreline.

3   pounds sirloin, sliced thin, any tender cut

$^1/_2$ cup flour

1   teaspoon salt

$^1/_2$ teaspoon pepper

$^1/_2$ cup olive oil

3   tablespoons butter

1   10-ounce package whole mushrooms, sliced

1   quart beef broth

6   ounces vinegar

$^1/_2$ teaspoon garlic salt

8   ounces sour cream

1   pound egg noodles, cooked according to package directions

Instructions:

Dredge sirloin in flour seasoned with salt and pepper. In a large skillet, melt oil and butter on medium heat. Sear the sirloin on both sides and add mushrooms. Cook this for 3-4 minutes on medium heat. Add beef broth and vinegar and bring to a boil. Reduce heat to simmer, add garlic salt and additional salt and pepper if needed. If the sauce appears too thin, add a flour/butter roux to thicken. Right before removing from heat, stir in sour cream and pour over cooked egg noodles.

Millionaire's Chow Mein

Shared by Hildye Cross, formerly of Greenwich

My mother took cooking classes from Libby Hillman many years ago. This is one of the recipes that I adopted from one of her cookbooks, with a couple of my own changes. It has become one of our family favorites! It's great when you're having friends for dinner and don't want to be stuck in the kitchen cooking!

2 tablespoons oil	$^1/_2$ cup bamboo shoots
2 teaspoons salt	$^1/_2$ cup water chestnuts, sliced
$1^1/_2$ pounds flank steak, sliced thin	$1^1/_2$ cups chicken broth
5 onions, chopped	1 teaspoon sugar
1 pound mushrooms, sliced	$1^1/_2$ teaspoons soy sauce
6 stalks celery, diced	4 tablespoons corn starch
$1^1/_2$ cups bean sprouts, drained	4 tablespoons water
	2 scallions, diced

Instructions:

In a large heavy skillet, heat oil and salt, add steak and quickly fry on both sides. Remove steak from skillet and transfer to a platter. Add onions to skillet and sauté until lightly browned. Add mushrooms and cook for 3 minutes until browned, add all remaining vegetables and cover with chicken broth. Cover and cook this mixture for a few more minutes. Add seasonings. Combine corn starch and water and add to saucepan to thicken the chow mein. Transfer the steak from the platter back into the saucepan, let this cook together for a couple of minutes. Garnish with scallions and serve with rice. This dish can be served right away or refrigerate it and reheated later.

Flank Steak with Tomatoes

Shared by Anne Rakocy, Madison

This is a great winter company meal since meat can be kept warm in the oven, while you are entertaining.

flank steak		3-5	tablespoons butter
flour		2	large onions, peeled, quartered & sliced
salt, to taste			
pepper, to taste		1	quart can stewed tomatoes

Instructions:

Preheat oven to 450-500 degrees. Season and flour steak on both sides. Place steak in a shallow roasting pan and dot with butter. Bake 5 minutes. When sizzling turn and bake 5 minutes more. Add onions and return to oven. Allow onions to soften and brown, 15–20 minutes. Mound onions on top of steak. Drain tomatoes, reserve juice. Mound tomatoes on top of onions. Reduce heat to 325 degrees. Bake for 1 hour basting occasionally with juices from pan and tomatoes. After 1 hour reduce heat further. Meat can be kept warm for a very long time.

Not Your Mama's Grilled Cheese Sandwich

Shared by Linda McIntyre, owner, The Villa Gourmet, Milford

2	slices of Tuscan round bread	1	thick slice brie cheese
1	tablespoon apple raisin based chutney	1	tablespoon carmalized onions
4	ounces sliced chicken breast, herb roasted	1	teaspoon Dijon mustard
			radicchio, optional

Instructions:

Be sure to use a nice fresh round of Tuscan bread, cut 2 thick slices. Coat one slice with the apple raisin chutney, top with sliced chicken breast. Best to use the herb roasted chicken already roasted from the grocery store. Place cheese on top of chicken and onions on top of cheese. Coat second piece of bread with Dijon mustard. Bring 2 pieces of bread together to form a sandwich and place in a Panini press for 2 minutes. Serve warm.

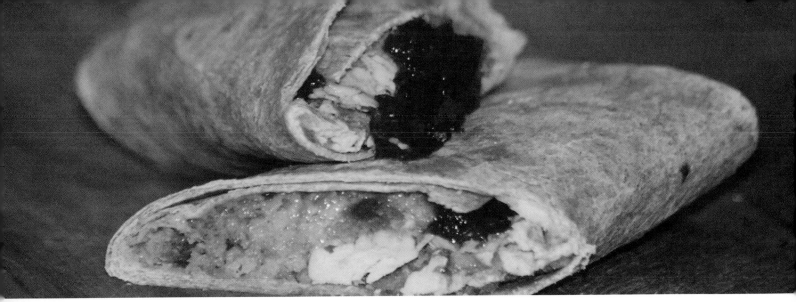

Thanksgiving Wrap

Shared by The Madison Coffee Shop, Madison

This is the perfect light meal to use with Thanksgiving leftovers!

1	teaspoon mayonnaise		1	tablespoon gravy
4	ounces turkey breast, freshly carved		1	tablespoon cranberry sauce
2	tablespoons stuffing		1	whole wheat wrap

Instructions:

Lay wrap flat and cover the whole surface with mayonnaise. Top with turkey, stuffing and cranberry sauce. Pour gravy on top and roll to close. Place wrap on a hot grill and heat for one minute to seal the ends closed.

Kristen's Mushroom Burgers

Shared by The Pantry, Fairfield

$^1/_2$ pound button mushrooms
$^1/_2$ pound portabello mushrooms
2   shitake mushrooms
1   tablespoon extra virgin olive oil
2   tablespoons butter
1   teaspoon parmesan cheese, grated
1   ounce cream cheese
6   cloves garlic, minced

$^3/_4$ tablespoon Dijon mustard
2   tablespoons Italian parsley, chopped
    pinch of nutmeg
1   ounce Panko breadcrumbs
    rolls

Optional:
    radicchio
    gorgonzola cheese, crumbled

Instructions:

Clean all mushrooms, trim/discard stems. Combine $^1/_4$ of each type of mushroom. Put in a food processor and chop fine. Slice remaining 75 percent of mushrooms into small pieces. In a large heavy skillet, heat oil and butter over medium heat and sauté all mushrooms (chopped and sliced). Let this cook down until all liquid is evaporated. Add the cheeses, garlic, mustard, parsley, nutmeg and breadcrumbs. Work this together and using a scoop, form the mixture into patties. Chill patties well. To serve, heat a non stick pan on medium high and sauté until burgers are cooked through. Top with arugala and crumbled gorgonzola cheese. Melt cheese topped burgers in the oven for 1–2 minutes and serve on a roll.

delicious desserts

GRANDMA'S BLUE RIBBON APPLE PIE

TWO LAYER BROWNIES

SYBIL'S BLUEBERRY COBBLER

CHOCOLATE MOCHA MOUSSE

HOT FUDGE SAUCE

APPLE CRISP

ITALIAN ALMOND MACAROONS

CRUNCHY FUDGE SANDWICHES

RIPPOWAN DINER RICE PUDDING

GRANDPA WILSON'S OATMEAL COOKIES

MYSTERY TARTE PIE

FRESH GINGER CAKE

FRENCH SILK PIE

DECADENT CHOCOLATE CAKE

PUMPKIN CAKE

APPLE BUNDT COFFEE CAKE WITH CARAMELIZED WALNUTS

STRAWBERRY CAKE

GEORGIA PECAN PIE

CARMEL–BANANA PIE

BONNIE'S PUMPKIN PIE

SWEDISH TORTE

BLUEBERRY CHEESE DELIGHT

APPLESAUCE CAKE

SCALLOPED APPLES

ITALIAN EASTER PIE

BAVARIAN APPLE TORTE

TORTA MIMOSA

NONNA CALABRO'S ESPRESSO RICOTTA CAKE

APPLE FRITTERS WITH BUTTERSCOTCH SAUCE

delicious desserts

Grandma's Blue Ribbon Apple Pie

Shared by Mark Castaldo, Madison

*As a young kid, I had a real aversion to apple pie, I remember
my mother chasing me around the house with a bite on a fork,
determined to get me to try it. It wasn't until I got older that
I learned to appreciate her apple pie which won several blue ribbons
at our local fairs in Middlebury, CT.*

8	macintosh apples, peeled and sliced	**Crust:**
1	cup sugar	2 cups flour
1	tablespoon cinnamon	$1/2$ cup oil
$1/2$	stick of butter, approximately	$1/4$ cup milk
1	teaspoon salt	1 teaspoon salt

Instructions:

Combine crust ingredients and roll out between wax paper to form 2 crusts.

Lay bottom pie crust in a pie plate. Put half of sliced apples into pie crust, sprinkle with $1/2$ cup sugar, and layer remaining apples on top of sugar. Sprinkle with remaining $1/2$ cup sugar, cinnamon, butter and salt. Put top pie crust on and make a few slits into the crust.

Bake for 15 minutes in a 425 degree oven, turn oven down to 350 and bake for another 45 minutes.

Two Layer Brownies

Shared by Nancy Lewis, owner, Sweet Rexie's, Norwalk

1 cup sugar	$^1/_2$ cup milk chocolate Chicago toffee, chopped
$^1/_2$ cup butter	
4 eggs, beaten	6 tablespoons butter
$^1/_2$ teaspoon salt	$^1/_2$ cup Sweet Rexie's chocolate covered pretzels broken into bite sized pieces
1 teaspoon vanilla	
1 cup flour	
1 16-ounce can Hershey's chocolate syrup	$^1/_2$ cup milk chocolate Chicago toffee, chopped
6 ounces semi-sweet chocolate chips	

Instructions:

In a large bowl, cream together sugar, butter and eggs. Add the salt, vanilla, flour, chocolate syrup and Chicago toffee pieces to bowl and beat well. Pour this batter into a greased 9 x 13 inch pan and bake for 30 minutes in a 350 degree oven. Let brownies cool completely. In a small saucepan heat semi sweet chocolate chips and butter. Pour this over brownies. Push bite sized pieces of chocolate covered pretzels into warm chip, butter layer. Finish these moist, decadent brownies by sprinkling another $^1/_2$ cup of Chicago toffee over top. Refrigerate until top layer hardens. Cut into brownie bars and store in tightly covered container.

Sybil's Blueberry Cobbler

Shared by Diane Gardner, Madison

This is truly a southern comfort food. Sybil was my Granny and she taught me to cook when I was a little girl. I have a collection of all of her recipes hand written by her. I use them all the time. She would sometimes make this with peaches, and she would always serve this hot out of the oven with a scoop of vanilla ice cream!

1 1/2	pints fresh blueberries	4	tablespoons baking powder
2	sticks butter, melted	1/2	teaspoon salt
2	cups sugar, divided		vanilla, to taste
1	cup milk	1	cup water
2	cups flour		

Instructions:

Line a 13x9 pan with blueberries. Combine melted butter, 1 cup of sugar, milk, flour, baking powder, salt and vanilla to make batter. Spread batter over blueberries. Combine remaining cup of sugar with water, mix to dissolve and pour over batter. Bake at 350 degrees for 1 hour or until bubbly and crispy, golden brown.

Chocolate Mocha Mousse

Shared by Ingrid Collins, owner, The Village Chocolatier, Guilford

4 tablespoons fresh brewed full bodied coffee	2 tablespoons butter
2 tablespoons sugar	2 teaspoons natural vanilla
6 ounces Cambra bittersweet chocolate, chopped	1 cup heavy cream mocha beans

Instructions:

Heat coffee and dissolve sugar into it. Place chopped chocolate in a medium sized bowl. Pour hot coffee/sugar over the chocolate. Cover and let sit for 30 seconds, until the chocolate is completely melted. Separate butter into small pieces and whisk into chocolate mixture one at a time. Add vanilla and let the mixture cool. Beat heavy cream in a chilled bowl until soft peaks form. Gently add small amounts of cream to chocolate mixture. When blended, gently fold remaining cream into the chocolate mixture. Spoon mousse into 4 martini glasses. Cover with plastic wrap and chill prior to serving. Top with shaved chocolate or mocha beans.

Cambra chocolate and mocha beans are available for sale at The Village Chocolatier and other fine candy stores along the shoreline.

Hot Fudge Sauce

Shared by Carolyn Sperry, formerly of Woodbridge

**Years ago, my neighbor, Tootie Beazley shared this recipe with me;
I have since shared it with all of my friends. Enjoy!**

1/4 cup butter	3/4 cup sugar
2 squares unsweetened chocolate (may substitute with sweetened chocolate)	1/2 cup evaporated milk
	1/2 teaspoon vanilla

Instructions:

Melt butter and chocolate over medium heat, add milk and sugar stirring constantly. Bring to a boil, remove from heat and whisk in vanilla.

Apple Crisp

Shared by Bishops Orchard, Guilford

8 apples, peeled, cored and sliced	$^1/_4$ cup corn starch
$^1/_2$ cup sugar	1 teaspoon cinnamon

Instructions:

Combine all ingredients, mixing well. Pour into an 8 inch square pan and top with apple crisp topping.

Topping

$^1/_2$ cup flour	$^3/_4$ cup rolled oats
$^1/_2$ cup brown sugar	$^1/_4$ cup butter
	1 teaspoon cinnamon

Instructions:

Blend together all ingredients, be careful not to over mix. The topping should be crumbly, spread over top of apple batter.

Bake for one hour in a 375 degree oven.

Italian Almond Macaroons

Shared by Peggy Antenucci, Madison

My maternal grandmother, Vera De Christofaro, came to the United States from Italy in 1910. Every holiday and family gathering, she baked cookies, and these almond macaroons became my favorite. For over twenty years I have been baking them for my family every Christmas.

2	cups granulated sugar	$^2/_3$	cup egg whites, slightly beaten
$^2/_3$	cup confectioners' sugar	1	pound almond paste
1	cup flour		pignoli nuts
$^1/_4$	teaspoon salt		maraschino cherries

Instructions:

Using a Kitchen Aid or similar mixer, blend sugars, flour, salt and egg whites. Cut almond paste into small pieces and add to mixer. Blend until all combined, dough will be sticky. Add a little flour if dough is too wet. Cherries should be cut in half and pat dry on a paper towel. Pat flour on hands and roll dough by spoonfuls into small balls. Place balls on cookie sheet lined with parchment paper. Press either a cherry half or a few pignoli nuts on top of each cookie.

Bake at 350 degrees fro 20–25 minutes until golden brown. Allow to cool before removing from paper. Store in air-tight tin.

Crunchy Fudge Sandwiches

Shared by Wendy W. Price, Madison

*My mother-in-law, Lois Price, gave this recipe to me 26 years ago.
I make them every year during the holidays and they have become a family
favorite. My two daughters, who are both in college now, make them for
their roommates, faculty and friends at their schools. They are delicious,
easy to make and relatively quick as there is no baking time involved.*

1	11-ounce package Nestle butterscotch morsels	1	cup confectioners' sugar, sifted
1	cup peanut butter	8	cups Rice Krispies
1	12-ounce package semi-sweet chocolate morsels	4	tablespoons butter
		2	tablespoons water

Instructions:

Melt butterscotch morsels with peanut butter over low heat, stirring until blended. Stir in Rice Krispies. Press half of this mixture into a buttered 13" x 9" oblong pan. Set aside and chill.

In a double boiler, melt chocolate morsels, confectioners' sugar, butter and water until all is melted and blended. Spread chocolate over chilled Rice Krispie mixture. Add a little water if needed to spread. Top with reserved Rice Krispie mixture. Chill and cut into squares and serve. *Enjoy!*

Rippowan Diner Rice Pudding

Shared by Don Knight, Stamford

This is my father's recipe he used to serve at his diner!

1	1 pound box Carolina rice	3	eggs, blended with a shot of milk
10	cups milk	1	15-ounce can fruit cocktail, drained
3	teaspoons vanilla	$^2/_3$	cup sugar
3	cups sugar	$^1/_3$	cup cinnamon
$1^1/_2$	teaspoons salt		
$^1/_4$	teaspoon nutmeg		
1	tablespoon butter		

Instructions:

Cook rice according to directions. Rice should be done in 4 minutes, remove rice and pour into strainer to remove excess water. Do not rinse rice.

Heat milk, vanilla, salt, nutmeg and butter in top of double boiler over medium heat. Pour rice into the milk mixture and stir for a very few minutes. The rice will begin to thicken after 25 minutes or so.

Now take the eggs and shot of milk and whip in a blender for 1 minute. Gently fold the egg mixture into the rice, stirring constantly. This will give it a custard like consistency. Add the fruit cocktail, mix well. Continue to cook until a large serving spoon will stand up in the rice pudding without falling over. It's done!

Put in decorative bowls, sprinkle the top with a mixture of sugar and cinnamon, to give it a brown, cinnamon flavored top. Serve chilled or room temperature.

Grandpa Wilson's Oatmeal Cookies

Shared by Liz Crowther, Madison

This is one of my Dad's (Stan Wilson) favorites. One of his most cherished Madison things to do, was to walk up town to the Hometown Bakery for the famous meltaways and doughnuts. He would then make deliveries along Middle Beach Road as he walked back home. No one else got up early enough to get the first ones out of the oven!

1^1/$_4$ sticks butter

1^1/$_4$ sticks margarine (Willow Tree Soy Margarine)

5 cups raw quick rolled oats

1 cup all purpose flour, sifted

2 teaspoons cinnamon

1 teaspoon salt

1 teaspoon baking soda

2 cups light brown sugar, packed, you can mix light and dark sugar

2 eggs, extra large

2 teaspoons vanilla

Optional:

raisins

Instructions:

Preheat oven to 375 degrees. In a large skillet, over medium heat, cook butter and margarine until lightly browned. Be careful not to burn. Add oats and sauté, stirring constantly until golden, about 5 minutes. Remove from heat and cool slightly.

Meanwhile, sift flour with cinnamon, salt and baking soda. Set aside. In a large bowl, combine sugar, eggs and vanilla. Beat until light. Add rolled oats and flour mixture, and stir until well combined.

Drop rounded teaspoons, 3 inches apart onto ungreased cookie sheet. A one inch ice cream scoop is the perfect size for this. I always use a silpat mat or parchment paper to line the cookie sheets. Bake 9-12 minutes or until golden. Transfer to wire rack and cool. Optional, you can add raisins.

Mystery Tarte Pie

Shared by Diane Gardner, Madison

My Aunt Jo Ellen gave me this recipe.
It is always a hit at any dinner party or gathering!

16   Ritz crackers, chopped
$^2/_3$ cup nuts, finely chopped
3   egg whites
$^1/_2$ teaspoon baking powder, sifted with
1   cup sugar
    vanilla, to taste
$^1/_3$ pint whipping cream

Instructions:

Combine finely chopped crackers and nuts together using a blender. In a separate bowl, beat egg whites until stiff, gradually adding baking powder and sugar. When whites are stiff, fold in nuts and crackers. Add vanilla and pour into greased 8 inch pie plate.

Bake at 350 degrees for 30 minutes. Cool before serving and serve with a dollop of fresh whipped cream. For an added touch, serve with some fresh raspberries or blackberries!

Fresh Ginger Cake

Shared by Aux Delices Foods, Stamford

1   cup sugar
4   ounces ginger, peeled and cut into small pieces
1   cup canola oil
1   cup molasses
1   cup boiling water
2   teaspoons baking soda
$^1/_2$ teaspoon cinnamon
$^1/_2$ teaspoon cloves, ground

$2^1/_2$ cups all purpose flour
2   eggs, beaten

Glaze:
1   cup confectioners' sugar
2-3 tablespoons heavy cream
$^1/_2$ cup ginger, crystallized, chopped

Instructions:

Preheat oven to 350 degrees, lightly grease a 9 inch cake pan and set aside. Process sugar and ginger in a food processor until it is very smooth and almost reaches a liquid consistency. Add the oil and molasses. In a separate bowl, combine the boiling water and baking soda and add it to the sugar and ginger mixture. Strain this mixture through a sieve to remove ginger fibers. Combine the spices and flour, and then slowly add the liquid mixture to the dry ingredients by hand with a whisk. Add the beaten eggs to the batter and pour the batter into the pan. Bake for about 20 minutes at 350 degrees, when the cake starts to rise, reduce the temperature to 320 degrees and continue cooking for another 20–25 minutes. Test the cake with a toothpick. Let the cake cool and then glaze or you can glaze it immediately and serve warm.

To prepare the glaze, combine the confectioners' sugar, and heavy cream in a small saucepan, heat on low for 10–20 seconds. Drizzle over the cake with a fork to make decorative lines, sprinkle crystallized ginger over top.

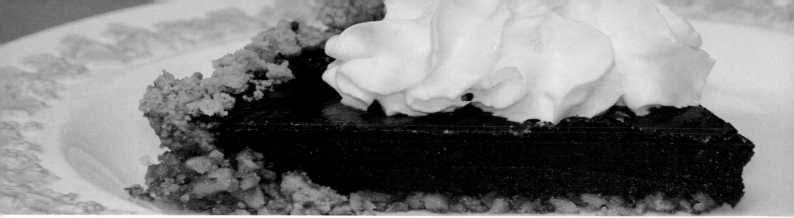

French Silk Pie

Shared by Kim Castaldo, Madison

*My children's fondest summer memories are renting homes on Nantucket.
After long, lazy afternoons at the beach, we would hop on our bikes
and peddle down to the Sconset Market and Café to see what tasty treats
had been prepared that day. This is one of our most loved recipes which
I have varied slightly from the original, which was published in the
Sconset Café cookbook.*

6	tablespoons butter	$^1/_8$	cup Kahlua
$4^1/_2$	sweetened baking chocolate squares	1	teaspoon vanilla
3	eggs		dash of salt
			whipped cream

Instructions:

In a heavy sauce pan, melt butter and chocolate until smooth, stirring constantly. Reduce heat to low and add eggs one at a time, whisking after each addition. Stir in Kahlua, vanilla and salt.

Pie crust

$1^1/_2$	cups walnuts	$^1/_4$	cup brown sugar, packed
		$^1/_3$	cup butter, softened

Instructions:

In a food processor, grind the nuts and sugar, be careful not to over grind and create a paste. Add butter until thoroughly combined. Spray 9 inch baking dish with cooking spray and press walnut mixture into bottom and onto sides of dish. Bake this for 10 minutes in a 350 degree oven until lightly browned. Cool in refrigerator for at least 30 minutes.

Pour chocolate mixture into pie crust and set in refrigerator for at least 6 hours to chill completely. Top with whipped cream.

Decadent Chocolate Cake

Shared by Karen Greenberg, Madison

Cake:

1 cup boiling water

3 ounces unsweetened chocolate

1 stick butter

1 teaspoon vanilla

2 cups sugar

2 egg yolks

1/2 cup sour cream

1 teaspoon baking soda

2 cups, plus 2 tablespoons flour

1 teaspoon baking powder

2 egg whites, beaten until stiff

Frosting:

2 tablespoons margarine

3/4 cup semi-sweet chocolate bits

6 tablespoons heavy cream

1 1/2 cups confectioners' sugar

1 teaspoon vanilla

Instructions:

Preheat oven to 350 degrees. Grease and flour spring form pan.

Place chocolate and butter in a bowl. Pour boiling water over chocolate/butter and let melt. Stir in vanilla and sugar. Wisk egg yolks and blend into chocolate butter mixture.

In a separate bowl, mix together sour cream and baking soda, whisk this into chocolate butter mixture. Add flour and baking powder, wisk these into batter. Beat egg whites until very still, stir half of egg whites into batter. Spoon remaining half of egg whites onto top of batter and gently fold into batter. Bake for 40–45 minutes.

Frosting:

Place all ingredients in a medium heavy sauce pan. Cook over low heat, whisking until very smooth. Let cake cool until slightly warm, pour warm frosting over cake to cover, it should look like a glaze.

Pumpkin Cake

Shared by Sherry Casagranda, Groton

This is my all time dearest holiday cake!

4 eggs, large	2 teaspoons baking soda
2 cups sugar	1 teaspoon salt
1$^{1}/_{3}$ cups canola oil	3$^{1}/_{2}$ teaspoons cinnamon
3 cups flour, sifted	1 14$^{1}/_{2}$-ounce can pumpkin
2 teaspoons baking powder	1 cup nuts, chopped

Instructions:

Beat eggs at high speed for 30 seconds, gradually adding sugar, beating until thick. In a slow, steady stream, add oil while blender continues to beat. At low speed, add sifted dry ingredients, alternating with pumpkin. Be sure to start with dry ingredients and end with dry ingredients, mixing until smooth. Stir in chopped nuts by hand. Pour into greased bundt cake pan. Bake at 350 degrees for 65 minutes, cool completely before removing from pan.

Cream Cheese frosting:

8 tablespoons cream cheese	3 cups confectioners' sugar
2 egg whites, beaten	1 teaspoon vanilla
	1 teaspoon salt

Instructions:

In a blender, beat cream cheese until soft. Add remaining ingredients and beat thoroughly. When cake is cooled, ice pumpkin cake and serve.

Apple Bundt Coffee Cake with Caramelized Walnuts

Shared by 3 Liberty Green, Clinton

✳

3	cups walnuts, chopped	1	stick butter, melted
1	cup maple syrup	2	eggs, beaten
2	cups white flour, unbleached	1	cup light brown sugar
2	teaspoons baking powder	1	cup sour cream, not light
1	teaspoon baking soda	1	cup macintosh apples, peeled,
	pinch salt		cored, seeded and sliced thin
$^1/_2$	teaspoon cinnamon		

Instructions:

In a small saucepan over medium heat, cook walnuts in maple syrup. Cook for 20–30 minutes until nuts absorb most of the liquid and it gets bubbly. In a large bowl, combine flour, baking powder, baking soda, salt and cinnamon. Blend well and set aside. In a separate bowl, combine butter, eggs and brown sugar. Add this wet mixture to the dry and blend well. Add sour cream and apples to combine, be careful not to over mix as this will make the coffee cake tough. Lightly oil (not butter) a 10 inch bundt cake pan and flour the bottom. Pour batter into pan and with a spatula cover the entire top surface with the chopped nuts. Bake for 45 minutes in a 350 degree oven. Allow the cake to cool for half an hour before slicing.

Strawberry Cake

Shared by Loretta Tallevast, Lake City , South Carolina

This is my grandchildren's favorite cake. They always ask me to make it every time I visit. It has now become their Birthday cake!

1 box white cake mix	$^3/_4$ cup Wesson oil
1 3-ounce package strawberry Jell-o	3 eggs
	$^1/_2$ cup frozen strawberries, thawed

Instructions:

Mix white cake mix with Jell-o and Wesson oil, add remaining ingredients and beat for 2 minutes. Divide batter into 3 greased cake pans and bake for 25 minutes at 350 degrees or until done.

Frosting:

1 stick butter, softened	$^1/_2$ cup frozen strawberries, thawed and mashed
1 box confectioners' sugar	fresh strawberries, to decorate

Instructions:

Cream butter and sugar and add strawberries and juice of berries. Let cake cool and frost. Keep in the refrigerator until ready to serve. Decorate with fresh strawberries and serve with vanilla ice cream.

Georgia Pecan Pie

Shared by Carol Kenyhercz, Branford

This is my number one pie...every Thanksgiving I bake about 10–15 of these pies and give them as gifts for my friend's holiday tables... people just rave about this pie. I received this recipe from a friend in Georgia about 40 years ago...its wonderful!

3	eggs	1	teaspoon vanilla
1/2	cup sugar	1	cup Karo corn syrup, light
4	tablespoons butter, melted	1 1/4	cups pecans, halved
1/2	teaspoon salt	1	unbaked pie shell, 8 inch

Instructions:

Beat eggs and sugar well in a bowl. Add melted butter, salt, vanilla and corn syrup. Fold in pecans. Pour into unbaked pie shell. Pecans will naturally float to the top when they are poured in the pie shell. Bake at 350 degrees for 55 minutes.

Carmel–Banana Pie

Shared by Josephine Redding, Stamford

My Mum used to make this for us when we were kids and now it is a favorite with our boys, who request it whenever we have family get togethers. I think this dish originated in Scotland.

✳

2	cans condensed milk	1	prepared pie crust
2	bananas	$^1/_2$	pint heavy cream

Instructions:

Put the two cans of condensed milk, UNOPENED, into a large saucepan (cooking pot). Cover with water and bring to a boil, then turn down to medium low and simmer for 3 hours. Keep adding water as it evaporates, the cans need to remain covered in water.

When the cans have simmered for 3 hours, remove from the water. Peel and slice bananas and arrange evenly over the pie crust. Open the cans of condensed milk that have now become caramel. Do this very carefully as the liquid is extremely hot. It is best to cover with a cloth as you open to avoid the liquid squirting onto hands or face.

Spoon the very thick caramel over the bananas and fill the pie crust. Leave to cool in the refrigerator. When the pie is chilled, whip the heavy cream to a thick consistency and spoon over the pie. Use a fork to create a decorative effect on the top of the pie by criss-crossing the cream.

It is important not to use a pre-sweetened cream because the caramel is very sweet.

Bonnie's Pumpkin Pie

Shared by Bonnie Risbridger, Madison
As Thanksgiving rolls around this is a favorite.

✳

$1^1/_2$	cups can pumpkin	$^3/_4$	teaspoon ginger
2	eggs, slightly beaten	$^1/_2$	teaspoon salt
1	tablespoon flour	$1^1/_2$	teaspoons molasses
$^3/_4$	cup sugar	1	ready made pie crust
$^3/_4$	cup milk		

Instructions:

Combine all ingredients together and pour into ready made pie crust. Bake at 375 degrees for about 40–45 minutes or until pie is set. Quick and easy.

Swedish Torte

Shared by Mary Perrotti, Middletown

*This is an old family recipe that we use for birthdays and anniversaries.
It was my father's favorite, when I got married it became my husband's
most sought after dessert and now our daughter, Carolyn,
looks forward to it every year on her birthday.*

¹/₂ cup butter	¹/₂ teaspoon baking powder
¹/₂ cup sugar, divided	¹/₂ teaspoon vanilla
4 eggs, divided	1 cup sugar
5 tablespoons cream or whole milk	4 tablespoons nuts, chopped
1 cup cake flour	1 cup whipped cream
	1 cup fruit of your choice

Instructions:

In a large bowl, cream together the butter and ¹/₂ cup sugar. Add egg yolks and beat 5-10 minutes until light and creamy, then add cream. Sift together flour and baking powder. Add this to the butter mixture and then add vanilla. Beat this very well. Grease and flour two round cake pans. Pour batter evenly between the 2 pans. In a separate bowl, beat together egg whites and 1 cup of sugar, pour this on top of butter batter. Sprinkle all chopped nuts on top of the batter in one of the cake pans. Bake for 35 minutes in a 325 degree oven. When ready to serve, remove cakes from pans (if they stick in the pans, heat slightly on stove top to loosen). Turn bottom layer upside down on cake plate and spread top with whipped cream and fruit. Top with second layer so that the crushed nuts are on the top of the torte.

Blueberry Cheese Delight

Shared by Lisa Kennally, Madison

*This has been a treasured family recipe since I was a young girl.
It's easy to make and delicious. Cherries or pineapples can be used
in place of the blueberries if desired.*

2	8-ounce packages cream cheese, room temperature	1	can blueberry pie filling
$2/3$	cup sugar	1	pint whipping cream
4	eggs	1	tablespoon confectioners' sugar
2	tablespoons vegetable oil	1	teaspoon vanilla extract

Instructions:

In a large bowl, beat together the cream cheese, sugar, eggs and oil. Pour this mixture into a 9 x 13 inch pan and bake for 20 minutes in a 325 degree oven. Remove from oven and be careful not to overcook. When cooled, top with can of blueberry pie filling. In a small bowl, whip cream, sugar and vanilla until lightly fluffy. Spread cream topping over blueberry mixture. Cut into squares and enjoy!

Applesauce Cake

Shared by Bishops Orchard, Guilford

⁎

$1/2$	cup shortening	$1^1/2$	teaspoons salt
2	cups sugar	$3/4$	teaspoon cinnamon
1	egg, extra large	$1/2$	teaspoon cloves
$1^1/2$	cups applesauce	$1/2$	teaspoon allspice
$2^1/2$	cups flour	$1/2$	cup apple cider
$1^1/2$	teaspoons baking soda	$1^1/2$	cups raisins

Instructions:

In a large bowl, cream together shortening, sugar, egg and applesauce. In a separate bowl, sift together flour, baking soda, salt, cinnamon, cloves and allspice. Combine wet and dry ingredients together and mix until well blended. Add apple cider and stir in raisins. Grease cake pan and bake for 45–50 minutes in a 350 degree oven.

Scalloped Apples

Shared by Lyman Orchards, Middlefield

Originally founded in 1741, Lyman Orchards is currently managed by John Lyman III, the ninth generation of Lyman's to run the farm. This recipe comes from Edna Lyman, John's grandmother, who served these apples at family gatherings and church picnics for many years.

⁎

$2^1/2$	cups water	3	tablespoons butter or margarine
$1/2$	cup sugar	$1/3$	cup lemon juice, fresh
6	baking apples, medium to large, peeled, cored and quartered	$1/2$	cup maple syrup

Instructions:

Preheat oven to 350 degrees. Butter a 9x13x2 baking dish. In a large saucepan, combine water, sugar and apples, bring to a boil and cook for one minute. Place apples rounded side up, in the prepared baking dish. Pour water/sugar cooking liquid over apples. Break butter or margarine into small pieces and sprinkle over apples. Pour lemon juice and then maple syrup over the apples. Bake for one hour until apples are tender.

Italian Easter Pie

Shared by Christine Chesanek, Old Saybrook

**This dish is a family tradition that I have since brought to my store,
"Fromage" to celebrate the Easter season.**

Pie crust:

2   cups flour

$^1/_2$ cup sugar

1   teaspoon baking powder

1   stick butter, unsalted,
room temperature

2   large eggs

2   tablespoons whole milk

Instructions:

Combine all ingredients in a food processor and pulse until mixture
forms a ball. Place on a floured surface and knead by hand into a more
uniformed ball then wrap in plastic wrap. Refrigerate for at least $^1/_2$ an
hour or more.

Pie Filling:

2   pounds ricotta cheese, fresh

6   eggs

$1^1/_2$ cups light cream

1   pinch fresh lemon zest

2   teaspoons real vanilla extract

1   cup sugar

2   tablespoons sugar, to make
cinnamon sugar for topping

Instructions:

Place all ingredients except the sugar and cinnamon for topping in a large
mixing bowl and stir well. Take refrigerated pie dough out and roll with a
rolling pin on a floured surface. Line a 10 inch pie plate with the dough
and crimp the crust. Pour filling into uncooked crust. Put pie into an
oven that has been preheated to 400 degrees. Bake for 15 minutes and
then lower the temperature to 350 degrees and bake for another 45 minutes. Pie is done when center of pie is firm to the touch. Cool on wire
rack and sprinkle with cinnamon sugar mixture in center of pie. This can
be refrigerated for up to 5 days.

Bavarian Apple Torte

Shared by Martha Hoffman, Madison

Crust:

$1/2$ cup butter

$1/3$ cup sugar

$1/4$ teaspoon vanilla

1 cup flour

Filling:

8 ounces cream cheese, room temperature

$1/4$ teaspoon cinnamon

$1/4$ cup sugar

1 egg

$1/2$ teaspoon vanilla

Apple Mixture:

4 cups granny smith apples, peeled, thinly sliced

$1/3$ cup sugar

$1/2$ teaspoon cinnamon

$1/4$ cup almonds, slivered

Instructions:

To make the crust, cream together the butter and sugar until light and fluffy. Blend in vanilla and flour, mix well. Spread this dough onto bottom and up to $1^1/2$ inches on the sides of a 9-inch spring form pan. In a medium bowl, combine the cream cheese, cinnamon and sugar until well blended. Mix in egg and vanilla and pour into the dough lined pan. In a separate bowl, toss apple slices with sugar and cinnamon. Spoon apple mixture over cream cheese layer and top with almonds. Bake in a 450 degree oven for 10 minutes, then reduce temperature to 400 degrees and continue baking for another 25 minutes. Loosen cake from rim of pan with a knife, cool and remove rim. Serve chilled.

This recipe serves 6–8.

Torta Mimosa

Shared by Laura Fratini, Terranova Bracciolini, Italy
My family and I were on vacation in Italy this summer, 2007.
We stayed in a fantastic Villa in Terranova Bracciolini in Tuscany.
One of the owners, Laura gave me and my daughters baking lessons.
This is one of the recipes that she shared with us.

3	egg yolks	1	tablespoon confectioners' sugar
3	egg whites	$^1/_2$	cup flour, plain
3	tablespoons boiling hot water	$^1/_4$	cup potato flour, starch
$^3/_4$	cup sugar	2	teaspoons yeast powder

Instructions:

Take egg yolks and add boiling water, beat 2–3 minutes until creamy, add $^1/_2$ tablespoon confectioners' sugar and $^2/_3$ cup sugar. Beat until creamy, set aside.

Next, beat egg whites until stiff and slowly add the remaining sugars. Gently fold in the yolk mixture from bottom to top using a wooden spoon. This preserves the air in the sponge cake. Add all flour and yeast and mix. Do not over mix.

Using parchment paper, line bottom of greased cake pan. Put mix into pan and smooth out. Bake for 30 minutes at 350 degrees or until done. Do not over cook. Let cool.

Filling:

1	pound mascarpone cheese	6	tablespoons sugar
4	eggs, separated		rum, to taste, enough to wet sponge cake (I used coconut flavored)

Instructions:

Whisk egg whites until fluffy. Set aside. Whisk yolks, add mascarpone cheese to yolk and add sugar. Mix, fold in whites. Filling is ready.

Cut sponge cake in half and remove some of the middle of cake, set aside. Splash cake with rum until soft. Ice cake generously. Crumble the left-over cake over the top and refrigerate until ready to serve.

Nonna Calabro's Espresso Ricotta Cake

Shared by Fiorella Cutrufello, Calabro Cheese, East Haven

Crust:

2 cups graham cracker crumbs

$1/2$ cup butter or margarine, room temperature

Filling:

$1^1/2$ tablespoons unflavored gelatin

3 tablespoons cold water

$1/2$ cup granulated sugar

1 cup double strength espresso coffee, brewed

2 pounds Calabro whole milk Ricotta cheese

1 teaspoon vanilla

1 cup heavy or whipping cream

2 tablespoons semi-sweet chocolate, grated

$1/8$ teaspoon ground cinnamon

Instructions:

Crust: Heat oven to 400 degrees. Mix graham cracker crumbs with butter. Press mixture evenly over bottom and 2- $2^1/2$ inches up the sides of a buttered 9-inch springform pan. Bake 5 minutes. Remove from the oven and place pan on a wire rack to cool completely.

Filling: In a small saucepan sprinkle gelatin over cold water and stir. Add sugar and espresso and stir 2-3 minutes over moderately low heat, until liquid is almost boiling and gelatin is completely dissolved. Remove from heat and cool about 5 minutes. In a large mixing bowl beat ricotta and vanilla for 5 minutes at medium speed, until very smooth. Slowly pour in cooled gelatin mixture, beat 3 more minutes.

In a medium bowl whip cream until soft peaks hold when beater is lifted. With a rubber spatula fold cream into ricotta mixture. Scrape cream into cooled crust. Cover and refrigerate 3 hours or up to 4 days. Before serving, remove sides of pan. Mix grated chocolate and cinnamon and sprinkle on top of cake.

Apple Fritters with Butterscotch Sauce

Shared by Bee and Thistle Inn, Old Lyme

2	cups flour, sifted	2	tablespoons butter, melted
2	tablespoons sugar, granulated	2	cups water
2	teaspoons baking powder	2	teaspoons lemon juice
1	teaspoon salt	2	apples, peeled and diced
2	eggs, separated	4	cups canola oil, for frying

Instructions:

In a large bowl, sift together dry ingredients. In a separate bowl, beat egg yolks very well. Combine egg yolks with dry ingredients and add butter, water and lemon juice and beat until smooth. In a small bowl, beat egg whites until stiff. Fold egg whites into batter and add diced apples mixing to coat. Drop apple mixture by spoonful into oil that has been heated to 350 degrees, medium high. Cook until delicate brown and drain on absorbent paper.

Butterscotch sauce		12	tablespoons butter, unsalted
$4^1/_2$ cups sugar, dark brown		3	cups whipping cream
$^3/_4$ cup water		3	tablespoons apple cider vinegar

Instructions:

Combine sugar and water in a heavy bottomed saucepan that holds at least $2^1/_2$ quarts. Stir over low heat until sugar dissolves then raise heat to medium and bring to a boil. Let mixture boil until it begins to smoke and thicken This will rise up in the pan and become foamy and start emitting puffs of smoke. Carefully drop in butter and stir until it dissolves. Stir in cream and return to boil. Turn off heat and stir in vinegar. Cool to lukewarm and serve immediately. Serve with the best vanilla ice cream you can find!!

KIDS IN THE KITCHEN

kids in the kitchen

Corn Chowder

Shared by Jesse Gardner, Madison
I make this for my family, it's a quick and delicious snack.

★

1	small red onion, chopped fine	3	tablespoons flour
$^1/_2$	red or yellow pepper, diced	1	14-ounce can of white and yellow corn, mixed
7-10	small red potatoes, washed and chopped	3	cups milk
4-5	tablespoons butter		salt, to taste
			pepper, to taste

Instructions:

Put the diced onion, peppers, potatoes and butter in large saucepan and cook over medium heat, stirring until potatoes are tender. Stir in the flour and cook for 2 minutes or until bubbly.

Add the can of corn with liquid and mix until smooth. Add 1 cup of milk at a time and continue stirring until smooth. Cook for 10–15 minutes until chowder begins to boil. Season with salt and pepper and simmer on very low heat for another 15 minutes. Be careful not to burn.

Homemade Salsa

Shared by Catherine Chatillon and Julie Castaldo, Madison

1 large tomato, chopped
1 small onion, chopped
$^1/_2$ small red pepper, chopped
$^1/_2$ small green pepper, chopped
$^1/_2$ small yellow pepper, chopped
2 ounces jarred roasted red peppers, chopped

$^1/_4$ cup tomato puree
2 tablespoons Red Rooster Hot sauce
2 tablespoons white vinegar
salt, to taste
pepper, to taste

Instructions:

Combine all ingredients in a medium sized bowl. Cover and refrigerate overnight and serve with your favorite tortilla chips!

Potato Pancakes

Shared by Jesse, Ty and Halle Gardner, Madison

2	large Idaho potatoes, peeled and quartered	salt, to taste
2	medium carrots, chopped	pepper, to taste
1	small onion, quartered	olive oil, for sautéing
1	large egg, beaten	butter, for sautéing
3	tablespoons flour	applesauce
	nutmeg, to taste	sour cream

Instructions:

In a food processor, grate potatoes, carrots and onions all together. Transfer to large mixing bowl. Using your hands, add egg, flour and nutmeg. Squeeze out excess juice and form patties.

Use enough butter and olive oil mixture to cover the bottom of large fry pan. Heat oil and butter and add potato pancakes when oil/butter is hot. Salt and pepper each potato pancake as it is frying. Fry until crispy and golden brown on both sides. Keep a platter in oven at 200 degrees to keep potato cakes warm while you continue to fry. Never cover potato cakes, the crispy edge will be lost. Serve immediately with a small bowl of applesauce and sour cream.

Asian Stir-fry

Shared by Lucas Gillespie, Guilford

steak, your favorite grill cut
broccoli, chopped in bite
size pieces
sweet white onion, diced
sweet potato, diced
carrots, diced
peppers, diced, optional
olive oil, for stir fry

Sauce:

1	cup coconut milk
$^1/_4$	cup pineapple juice
	handful cilantro, chopped
$^1/_4$	teaspoon coriander
$^1/_4$-$^1/_2$	teaspoon fresh ginger, minced

Instructions:

Cut the first 6 ingredients into bite size pieces and set aside. Keep the steak pieces in a separate bowl. Combine all ingredients for the sauce and mix well. Pour $^1/_2$ sauce over the steak and let marinate.

Using olive oil in your wok, stir fry broccoli until it is just beginning to get tender, add sweet potatoes and carrots, once they are tender add onion, as onion is becoming soft, add steak and cook to desired doneness.

Once steak is cooked the way you like it, pour remaining sauce and mix into the ingredients and let sit for a few minutes. *Enjoy!*

Jake's Pan Fried Noodles

Shared by Jake Esposito, Madison

Kids love to make and eat these noodles. They are FUN to eat with chop sticks!

$1/2$ pound egg noodles or spaghetti, cooked al dente
salt

1 pound chicken breast, boneless and skinless, cut in $1/2$ inch strips

1 bunch scallions, sliced

3 tablespoons fresh ginger, finely chopped

2 garlic cloves, finely chopped

5-6 tablespoons peanut oil

$1/2$ teaspoon red chili flakes

4 tablespoons soy sauce

2 tablespoons fresh lemon juice

Instructions:

Using a wok or large skillet, coat bottom of pan with 4 tablespoons of peanut oil, add chicken and stir fry on high for 1-2 minutes. Push chicken aside, add a little oil to middle and stir fry scallions, ginger, garlic and chili flakes. Add the last drops of oil to pan along with the noodles stirring 1 minute and add soy sauce and lemon juice. Toss altogether and serve immediately.

Night before French Toast

Shared by Ty Gardner, Madison

3 eggs

$1/3$ cup milk, low fat

$1/2$ teaspoon vanilla

$1/4$ teaspoon cinnamon
pinch nutmeg

2 slices thick bread, white or whole wheat
fresh berries, any kind

1-2 tablespoons honey or your favorite syrup

Instructions:

Whisk together eggs, milk, vanilla, cinnamon and nutmeg. Lightly spray a small casserole dish with non stick cooking spray. Lay bread slices on bottom of casserole. Bread should fit snug in baking dish. Pour $1/2$ egg mixture over the bread, turn over and pour the rest on the other side.

Cover casserole and refrigerate overnight. Place in oven and bake for 20–25 minutes at 325 degrees or until light brown. Serve with fresh berries and honey.

Deviled Eggs

Shared by Jesse Gardner, Madison

This is one of my favorite snack foods.

✳

Instructions:

Put eggs into saucepan, fill with cold water and bring to a boil on medium heat. Let boil for 5–7 minutes, turn stove off and let cool. Run eggs under cold water while you peel off shells. Slice eggs in half, lengthwise. Remove yolks, put in bowl. Mash yolks, add mayonnaise and mustard. Season with salt and pepper. Stuff each egg white with yolk mixture and sprinkle with paprika.

1 dozen eggs
$^1/_2$ cup mayonnaise
3 teaspoons Dijon mustard
salt, to taste
pepper, to taste
paprika

Jesse's Cheese Quesadillas with Onions

Shared by Jesse Gardner, Madison

This is one of my specialties. I made this as a surprise for my Mom and Dad's Anniversary dinner.

5	tablespoons butter	2	dollops sour cream
4	10 inch flour tortillas		lettuce, chopped
1	cup Mexican cheese, shredded		tomatoes, chopped
1/2	small Vidalia onion, thinly sliced	3	tablespoons jarred salsa

Instructions:

Melt half of the butter in fry pan, place one tortilla in butter and fill with 1/2 of the cheese and 1/2 of the onions. Add another tortilla on top and lightly brown on one side. Flip and lightly brown on the other side. Repeat with the other 2 tortillas.

Slice the quesadillas with a pizza slicer and serve with sour cream, lettuce, tomato and salsa. Variations include diced chicken, black olives, avocado or any topping that you like!

Connor's Crazy Crackers

Shared by Connor Castaldo, Madison

*This is my favorite after school snack
and my mom says it is healthy, too!*

6	Ritz whole wheat crackers	6	raisins
1/2	slice American cheese	2	granny smith apple slices
2	teaspoons peanut butter		

Instructions:

On a small plate, put 2 crackers side by side. Top each cracker with 1/3 piece of American cheese, top each piece of cheese with another cracker. Top these crackers with one teaspoon of peanut butter, put 3 raisins onto each peanut butter cracker. Put another cracker on top of each peanut butter/raisin cracker and top with a slice of green apple.

Johnny's Pesto Pasta

Shared by Johnny Castaldo, Madison

1	bunch fresh basil	parmesan cheese, to taste
1/4	cup olive oil	salt, to taste
1/4	cup pignoli nuts	pepper, to taste
1	tablespoon garlic, crushed	
1	pound spaghetti, cooked al dente	

Instructions:

Put the first 4 ingredients in a food processor and puree until well blended. Cook pasta and rinse with water. Coat pasta with pesto and season with salt and pepper. Top with parmesan cheese and serve!

Salade De Luca

Shared by Lucas Gillespie, Guilford

1 bag Organic mix of lettuce, *"Two Guys from Woodbridge"* has a fantastic just picked mix pea shoots

1 Asian pear

1 slice of lemon

¼ cup goat cheese with herbs raspberry dressing, I like Drew's

Instructions:

Wash and spin lettuce and shoots well. Slice up Asian pear and sprinkle with a bit of lemon juice on the slices to prevent browning. Add the pear slices to the lettuce mix. Crumble goat cheese on top of salad. Add raspberry dressing to taste, mix gently…*Yummy!*

Bruschetta

Shared by Lucas and Chloe Gillespie, Guilford

  your favorite Ciabatta, We like Chabaso Bakery's

  extra virgin olive oil

  balsamic vinegar

  lettuce, shredded

1 fresh garlic clove, minced

  small white onion, diced

  orange or yellow pepper, diced

  sausiscon (sliced salami), shaved

  pepper, to taste

  salt, to taste

  parmesan cheese, shaved

Instructions:

Slice up the Ciabatta loaf. Lightly drizzle olive oil and balsamic vinegar on each slice. Top with shredded lettuce, garlic, onion and pepper. Then top with a little salami and shaved fresh parmesan cheese. Season to taste with a pinch of salt and pepper.

Arrange on a nice serving platter and EAT!!

Sticky Chicky Wings

Shared by Halle Gardner, Madison

1	pound chicken wings, drumettes and wings	honey, to taste
1	cup bar-be-cue sauce	salt, to taste
		pepper, to taste

Instructions:

Wash chicken and place in 9 x 13 casserole dish. Brush bar-be-cue sauce all over chicken and drizzle with honey. Season with salt and pepper and bake at 400 degrees for about 1 hour or until wings are turning crispy and tender.

Overnight Sausage Soufflé

Shared by Alison Lamothe, Madison

1 pound sausage links,
  maple flavored works best
4 eggs, beaten
2 cups milk
$^{1}/_{2}$ teaspoon salt
6 white bread slices, cubed
1 cup grated cheddar cheese

Instructions:

Cook the sausage according to package directions. In a small bowl, beat the eggs, milk and salt until well blended. Butter a $2^{1}/_{2}$ quart casserole dish and alternate layers of bread, grated cheese and sausage. Once you have finished layering, pour the egg mixture over the layers. Cover and refrigerate overnight. Bake covered for 45–50 minutes in a 325 degree oven. Remove cover for last 5–10 minutes to brown the top.

I have no idea where this recipe came from except that my entire family on my Mom's side has been making this for years on Christmas day and for Easter brunch. Trust me, I am not an egg fan, but I love this dish because it doesn't have the same texture that most egg dishes have. I guarantee you will love it!

Carolyn's Favorite Smoothie

Shared by Carolyn Castaldo, Madison

$^1/_2$ cup skim milk

$^1/_2$ cup Minute Maid orange
    juice blends

1 small banana

5 whole strawberries, frozen

2 ice cubes

Instructions:

Put all ingredients in a blender and mix until completely smooth.
Serve cold with a straw. For an extra boost, add some vitamin C powder!

Southern Banana Pudding

Shared by Halle Gardner, Madison

2   boxes cook and serve vanilla pudding

1   box Nilla wafers

4   bananas, ripe and sliced
     Cool Whip

Instructions:

Cook pudding according to instructions on package. In an air tight container, layer cookies, bananas and pudding. Continue to layer and top with Nilla wafers. Top with Cool Whip and refrigerate. *Enjoy!*

Ty's Original S'mores

Shared by Ty Gardner, Madison

1	graham cracker, halved	chocolate syrup
1	large marshmallow	

Instructions:

Top cracker with marshmallow and drizzle chocolate syrup and microwave for 5–10 seconds. Top with other half of cracker and dig in! Quick and easy to make.

Julie's Jell-o Cups

Shared by Julie Castaldo, Madison

1	package instant cherry Jell-o	Reddi-wip cream
1	package instant orange Jell-o	

Instructions:

Make both boxes of Jell-o according to package instructions. Spray Pam on mini cupcake tray. Fill each cupcake mold to the brim with Jell-o.

Refrigerate for several hours. When completely jelled, remove Jell-o from tins and decorate with a dollop of whipped cream on each. Serve chilled and eat up!

Frozen Mini Key Lime Pies

Shared by Julie Castaldo, Madison

4 large egg yolks	$^1/_2$ cup lime juice, fresh
$^1/_4$ cup sugar	green food coloring
1 14 ounce can sweetened condensed milk	1 package prepared mini graham cracker crusts, package of 6
2 tablespoons lime zest, grated	1 can Reddi-wip cream

Instructions:

Blend together egg yolks, sugar, condensed milk, lime zest and lime juice. Add one drop of food coloring to make yellow mixture turn green. Pour mixture into each of the 6 pie crusts.

Freeze for at least 4 hours. Remove from freezer and spray whipped cream on top of each pie.

Peanut Butter Cookies

Shared by Ashely, Amber and Britt Gardner, Guilford

¹/₂ cup butter	¹/₂ teaspoon baking powder
¹/₂ cup peanut butter	³/₄ teaspoon baking soda
¹/₂ cup brown sugar	1 teaspoon vanilla
1 egg	2 tablespoons milk
1¹/₄ cups flour	¹/₂ cup sugar for rolling

Instructions:

Mix together butter, peanut butter and brown sugar. Add egg, flour, baking powder, baking soda, vanilla and milk. Roll dough into small balls. Roll each ball into sugar and place on greased cookie sheet. Press tops of each cookie with a fork to flatten slightly. Bake at 375 degrees for 8–10 minutes.

Warm Fiesta Dip

Shared by Jesse and Brooke Esposito

***Bring a copy of this recipe wherever you go
because everyone asks for the recipe!!***

2 8-ounce packages cream cheese	2 cans Hormel chili, beans optional
2 bunches scallions, diced	2 8-ounce packages monterey jack cheese, shredded
2 cans black olives, sliced	
2 small jars pepperoncini, drained and chopped	

Instructions:

Preheat oven to 350 degrees. Layer in 13 x 9 pan in order topping off with cheese. Bake uncovered for 25–30 minutes. Serve with nachos or Fritos scoops.

Pumpkin Chocolate Muffins

Shared by Alison Lamothe, Madison

*I first had these muffins at our family's cabin in Bartlett, NH.
My grandma had made them and I remember thinking that
they were the best things since chocolate. I was and still am,
quite a chocolate fan, for me it was a big thing to love something
more than my beloved chocolate.*

$1^2/_3$ cups flour	2 large eggs
1 cup sugar	1 cup plain pumpkin
1 tablespoon pumpkin pie spice	$^1/_2$ cup butter, melted
1 teaspoon baking soda	1 cup chocolate chips, mini
$^1/_4$ teaspoon salt	$^1/_2$ teaspoon almond extract
$^1/_4$ baking powder	

Instructions:

Thoroughly mix flour, sugar, spice, baking soda, baking powder and salt in a large bowl. In a separate bowl, beat together eggs, pumpkin and butter. Stir in the chocolate chips and almond extract. Fold the wet ingredients into the dry until well blended. Be sure not to over blend or the muffins will turn out too hard. Scoop batter evenly into muffin tins lined with paper liners. Bake for 20–25 minutes in a 350 degree oven. Muffins should be puffed and springy to the touch. They taste best when wrapped in plastic wrap and eaten the following day.

Butterscotch Pumpkin Muffins

Shared by Holly and Dylan Edwards, Madison

$1^3/_4$ cups flour

$^1/_2$ cup brown sugar, packed

$^1/_2$ cup sugar

$^1/_2$ teaspoon ginger, ground

$^1/_2$ teaspoon mace, ground

$^1/_8$ teaspoon cloves, ground

1 teaspoon baking soda

$^1/_4$ teaspoon baking powder

1 teaspoon cinnamon

2 eggs

1 can pumpkin

1 stick butter, melted

1 cup butterscotch chips

Instructions:

In a large bowl, mix together flour, sugar, spices, baking soda and baking powder. Create a well in the middle of dry ingredients. In another bowl whisk together eggs, pumpkin and butter. Stir in chips. Pour egg mixture into well in large bowl, fold together just until moistened. Be sure not to over mix. Spoon mixture into greased muffin tins and bake for 20–25 minutes in a 350 degree oven. If you are using mini muffin trays, bake for 10 minutes.

This recipe makes 18 large or 36 mini muffins.

Chocolate Fruit Skewers

Shared by Carolyn Castaldo, Madison

2	Hershey milk chocolate candy bars	10	large, fresh strawberries
2	bananas	10	wooden skewers

Instructions:

Heat candy bars in a double broiler until melted. Cut bananas into 10 thick pieces. Skewer 1 banana piece and 1 strawberry onto each skewer and dip into melted chocolate.

Line cookie sheet with wax paper and refrigerate skewers until chocolate hardens. *Enjoy!*

Ultimate Ice Cream Sandwiches

Shared by Austyn Cwiertniewicz, Branford

1	package (16 ounce) Nestle Toll House Ultimate cookie dough bar	3	cups vanilla or chocolate ice cream, slightly softened
		$^1/_2$	cup Nestle semi-sweet chocolate morsels

Instructions:

Prepare cookie dough according to package directions. Cool cookies and remove from cookie sheet. Place $^1/_2$ cup of ice cream on the flat side of one cookie, top with flat side of second cookie to make a sandwich. Roll open sides of sandwich in morsels to coat. Wrap tightly in plastic wrap and freeze for at least one hour before serving.

Fun Pizza

Shared by St. Andrews Nursery School, Madison, Class of '05–'06

$3^1/_2$	cups flour	1	cup prepared tomato sauce
4	tablespoons shortening	1	cup mozzarella cheese, shredded
4	tablespoons butter	2	tablespoons olive oil
$^1/_2$	cup water		

Instructions:

Mix together first 4 ingredients, knead by hand. Stretch dough out by hand to fit onto a greased cookie sheet.

Spread sauce over dough and top with cheese. Drizzle with olive oil and bake for approximately 15 minutes at 475 degrees.

Nana's Chocolate Christmas Cookies

Shared by Hayley Cashman, Guilford

When my Mom was growing up, every year, the beginning of December, Nana would start the annual tradition of baking Italian chocolate cookies, also known as "Toto". Back before the convenience of food processors, she would work on collecting the ingredients and chopping them by hand, and baking the cookies in batches over several days. When they were baking, the whole house smelled like Christmas. She would then hide the cookies in different places throughout the house because otherwise, my Mom and Uncle Greg would devour them before Christmas ever came. Every year, they would search the house for the new cookie hiding places.

My Mom and I continue the tradition of Nana's Christmas cookies every year and it is a favorite holiday treat.

3	eggs	1	teaspoon nutmeg
³/₄	cup sugar	¹/₄	cup dates, chopped
¹/₂	cup Mazola oil	¹/₄	cup cherries, chopped
1	teaspoon vanilla	¹/₄	cup raisins
1	shot whiskey	³/₄	cup walnuts, chopped
1	medium orange, rind and juice	¹/₄	cup chocolate bits
¹/₄	teaspoon salt	4	teaspoon baking powder
1	teaspoon cloves	4	cups flour, unsifted
1	teaspoon cinnamon	¹/₄	cup cocoa
		1	small can Hershey's syrup

Instructions:

Combine eggs, sugar and oil into large bowl. In a separate bowl, beat vanilla, whiskey, orange rind and juice of orange until well blended. Add this mixture to large bowl and add salt, spices, fruits, nuts, baking powder, flour, and cocoa. Mix by hand until well blended. Add syrup and continue to mix.

Be sure to continuously dab oil on your hands to mold the cookies. Cookies should be about 1–2 inches in diameter, drop on cookie sheet, not too close as they rise and spread. Bake at 375 degrees for 10 minutes. Cookies are best glazed with chocolate icing!

Stack'em up Pancakes!

Shared by Halle Gardner

**My family loves when I make these on a Saturday
or Sunday morning for breakfast!**

2	cups all-purpose flour	1¹/₂	teaspoon vanilla
2	teaspoons sugar	4	tablespoons butter, melted
2	teaspoons baking powder	2	tablespoons butter, cold for
¹/₂	teaspoon salt		cooking
2	large eggs		chocolate chunks, optional
2¹/₂	cups buttermilk		

Instructions:

Mix all ingredients together, except the last 2 tablespoons of cold butter. Do not put chocolate chunks in batter. Melt butter in large fry pan and pour batter into the size you want pancakes to be. If making chocolate chunks pancakes, once the pancake starts to bubble a little, add chunks of chocolate to each pancake. When pancake is bubbling, flip and cook on other side for 1–2 minutes. Serve with your favorite syrup!

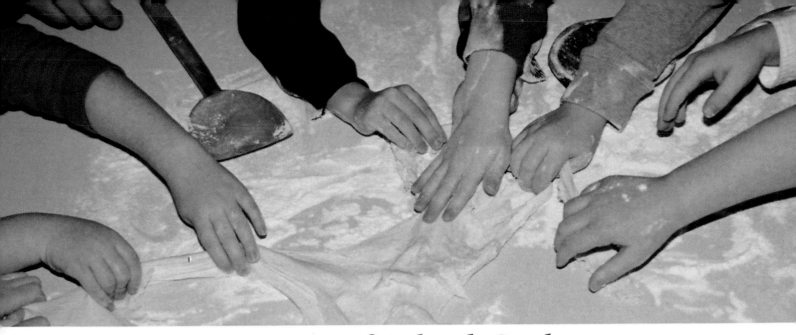

First Day of School Cookies

Shared by Cindi Gardner, Guilford

Being a single mom and a teacher, the first day of school was very frantic for my three daughters and myself. A couple days before school, I would make this batter and refrigerate it. I would purchase all of my daughter's favorite goodies for decorating. At the end of the first day of school, we would sit around the table and bake cookies and decorate them. We shared the day's events with one another. What a sweet way to start the school year off!

$^3/_4$ cup sugar	**Goodies:**
$^3/_4$ cup brown sugar	chocolate chips
1 egg	M&M's
2 cups flour	Snickers
$^1/_2$ teaspoon baking soda	raisins
1 teaspoon vanilla	coconut
1 cup butter	marshmallows

Instructions:

Blend both sugars and egg, add all the remaining ingredients. Roll dough onto floured surface. Cut into shapes using cookie cutters. Decorate with goodies before baking. Bake at 350 degrees for 8–10 minutes.

Gingerbread Cookie People

Shared by Susan Ciotti Wivell on behalf of Red Barn Nursery and Linda Stuhlman, Killingworth

A holiday favorite and a long time tradition of the Red Barn, the kids make these every year!

$5^1/2$	cups flour, unbleached
1	teaspoon baking soda
1	teaspoon salt
2	teaspoon ginger
2	teaspoons cinnamon
1	teaspoon cloves, ground
1	cup shortening
1	cup sugar
$1^1/4$	cups molasses
2	eggs, beaten

Instructions:

Thoroughly mix flour, soda, salt and spices and set aside. Melt shortening in a large saucepan and add sugar, molasses and eggs, mix well. Cool slightly, then add dry ingredients and mix well. Turn mixture onto a floured surface and knead. Roll dough to $1/8$ inch thickness and cut with people shape cookie cutters. Place on a greased cookie sheet.

Bake at 375 degrees for 8-10 minutes. Let cool for a few minutes on cookie sheet before moving to a cooling rack. Cookies can be decorated with raisins, M&M's and sprinkles before baking.

Great Great Aunt Ruthie's O'Henry Bars

Shared by Sarah and Hannah Johnson, Guilford

These yummy, gooey, chocolaty treats are an old-fashioned, home-made version of the granola bar. This recipe has been handed down in our family, Sarah and Hannah are probably the 5th or 6th generation of O'Henry Bar addicts! They are easy for kids to make and always a hit at bake sales and for camp care packages. The amount of chocolate chips can be increased if you're a real chocolate fan!

²/₃ cup butter

4 cups quick oats, Quaker is best

¹/₂ cup white Karo syrup

1 cup brown sugar

3 teaspoons vanilla

Topping:

12 ounces chocolate chips

³/₄ cup peanut butter, crunchy

Instructions:

In a large skillet, melt butter over medium heat and stir in remaining ingredients. Press oat mixture into a greased 9 x 13 inch pan and bake for 17 minutes in a 350 degree oven. Let this cool. While oat mixture is baking, melt chocolate in a pan on the stove or in the microwave. When melted, stir in peanut butter. Spread chocolate mixture onto cooled oat mixture, let chocolate set and cut into squares or bars. Yum!

INDEX

ACKNOWLEDGEMENTS

We dedicate this book to our family and friends that were so supportive to us once again as we compiled our 2nd book. We would like to send a special thanks to everyone that took the time to sit and write out their favorite recipes as well as sharing family stories and traditions.

This book would not be complete without thanking our husbands, their patience and support are so appreciated! We are more than grateful to our parents, Loretta Tallevast and Phyllis and John Carroll, for their advice, guidance and unending enthusiasm for our second cookbook.

Thank you to Kelley McMahon for her beautiful photography and keen eye once again. Thank you to Ty Gardner who made the sign that represents all of the towns that are included in our book. And a very special thanks to Christopher Devlin Photography and Carolyn Castaldo who also contributed to our collection of beautiful photographs. And last, but not least, to our wonderful graphic designer, Tammy Vaz, for her eye for detail as well as incredible creativity as you have seen throughout this book.

Finally, thank you to our children, who continue to inspire us each and every day!

CONNOR, TY, JESSE, HALLE, JULIE, CAROLYN, JOHNNY

Our kids
Our inspiration

What's Cooking?

MADISON

STONINGTON

STAMFORD

MYSTIC

CLINTON

OLD LYME

Guilford

Branford

OLD SAYBROOK

MILFORD

WESTBROOK

NORWALK

Bridgeport

WESTPORT

DARIEN

GREENWICH

Sign created by Ty Gardner